W9-BAE-721

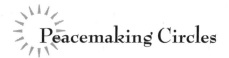 Peacemaking Circles

Vine Deloria, Jr., Reflects on Circles

The book *(Peacemaking Circles)* reminds me of the way that the Plains Indians often settled their disputes. A council would meet and discuss the nature of the problem, or crime, and every one would speak to the issue. Then elders would ponder the problem for a long time—unless it was a particularly heinous crime—and finally a solution would be found. The elders, of course, always sat in a circle to remind people that we are all equals and all participants. I think that format was probably used by most tribal people. I can't imagine a select group hearing a dispute and then rendering a quick judgment without causing great disruption in the community.

The circle eliminates the feeling of institutional coercion and enables people who have been injured to heal themselves and also places the offender in a position where, to keep any sense of personal integrity, he or she has to live up to community standards. Everyone learns from the experience. Contrast that with our procedures today where the family of the injured person gets a chance to curse the offender after the person has been convicted and the family is further encouraged to announce publicly that they have been partially revenged. Here no one learns anything, and the courtroom becomes merely an arena for institutionalized vengeance.

A powerful thinker who has spent his life on the cutting edge of justice in the broadest sense—encompassing cultural critique, change, and transformation—Vine Deloria, Jr., is the Professor Emeritus of History and Religious Studies at the University of Colorado in Boulder. Over decades, he has written on Native American life and history as well as on analyzing society and culture. His books include *Singing for a Spirit, Spirit and Reason, God is Red, For This Land, Red Earth, White Lies,* and *Custer Died for Your Sins.*

Participants Reflect on Circles

As a survivor of violence, this is the first thing that really resonated.

—A victim

I thought it would be easier. I didn't want to go to jail. I thought the Circle would give me an easier sentence. It was anything but easier, but it got me to where I am today, and jail wouldn't have done that. What is scary is that if I'd known—really known—how tough it was going to be in Circle, I'd have gone to court and gone to jail, and, this is the scary part, where would I be now?

—A former offender

This Circle work is about empowering people of color. . . . It seems to me that this process works best for those who have been oppressed the most. It gives them an option to make a difference in their communities—a process to begin healing.

—Circle trainer Gwen Chandler-Rhivers,
Minneapolis, Minnesota

Circles are so life-affirming—people coming together to make it work. They're the most powerful experience of community. I feel so connected to community in them. It doesn't seem to matter if people know each other when they come in.

—A community volunteer

The biggest gift we can give the community and the people we serve is the opportunity to resolve these problems themselves.

—Paul Schnell, St. Paul Police Department,
St. Paul, Minnesota

Practicing social democracy: that's what I contend Circles are.

—Darrol Bussler, Founder of South St. Paul
Restorative Justice Council,
St. Paul, Minnesota

Peacemaking Circles

From Crime to Community

KAY PRANIS
BARRY STUART
MARK WEDGE

LIVING JUSTICE PRESS
2003

Living Justice Press
St. Paul, Minnesota 55105

Copyright © 2003 by Kay Pranis, Barry Stuart, and Mark Wedge
All rights reserved. Published 2003
First edition

Printed in the United States of America

For information about permission to reproduce selections from this book, please write to:
Permissions, Living Justice Press, 2093 Juliet Avenue, St. Paul, MN 55105

Publisher's Cataloguing-in-Publication
(Provided by Quality Books, Inc.)

Pranis, Kay.
  Peacemaking circles : from crime to community / by
Kay Pranis, Barry Stuart, & Mark Wedge. — 1st ed.
  p. cm.
  Includes bibliographical references and index.
  LCCN 2003105933
  ISBN 0-9721886-0-6
  1. Community-based corrections. 2. Criminal justice,
Administration of—Citizen participation. 3. Restorative justice.
4. Healing circles. I. Stuart, Barry.
II. Wedge, Mark. III. Title.
HV9279.P73 2003   364.6'8
                    QBI03-200440

08 07 06 05 04   5 4 3 2

This book is printed on recycled, acid-free, elemental-chlorine-free paper.

Editor's note:
Because honoring confidentiality is an essential guideline of Circles, all names
and identifying circumstances have been altered or omitted throughout the
book, unless specific permission has been given otherwise.

Cover design by David Spohn
Interior design by Wendy Holdman
Composition at Stanton Publication Services, Inc., St. Paul, Minnesota

All excerpts from the unpublished report, *Holding the Space: The Journey of
Circles at Roca* by Dr. Carolyn Boyes-Watson, copyright © 2002, are reprinted
by permission of Carolyn Boyes-Watson.

WE AT LIVING JUSTICE PRESS are most deeply grateful to the Fund for Nonviolence (Santa Cruz, California) for their grant— our first and one that surpassed our hopes—as well as to Mary Joy Breton, Sister Pat Thalhuber, and Barbara Gerten for their individual donations. Their combined generosity and faith in our vision has made it possible for us to launch our press, which is devoted to the grassroots restorative justice movement, with the publication of this book.

To my children, Kevin Pranis, Laryssa Pranis, and Eva Pranis,
who made it possible for me to open myself
to unexpected dimensions of life

—KAY PRANIS

To my mother, Helen Fyfe Stuart,
whose humanity spoke through her warmth, intelligence,
and unswerving belief in the goodness within all people

—BARRY DRUMMOND NORMAN FYFE STUART

To Baha'u'llah for his sacred teachings that provided me with
guidance and direction, and to my mother, whose patience and
gentle teachings prompted me to try to understand the sacred

—MARK WEDGE

Contents

Preface

W E HAVE WRITTEN THIS OVERVIEW of how peacemaking Circles can be used with the justice system to share what we have learned from hundreds of Circles dealing with all types of crimes and crises. Circles are not, however, limited to these uses. In addition to bringing transformation in cases involving extreme violence and death, Circles work magic in families, schools, businesses, and communities, in other words, in meeting the challenges of everyday life. In this book, we focus on the criminal justice application of Circles. We offer our experiences to support the work that many pioneering community members and criminal justice professionals are doing around the world to explore a more healing, constructive response to crime.

Spaces ancient and modern. Peacemaking Circles are ancient spaces, recurring in various forms in many cultures. Probably our ancestors gathered in a circle around a fire, just as families gather around the kitchen table today. Long before we delegated our conflicts to experts, we came together in ancient peacemaking spaces to work through our differences and to make decisions toward the common good. William Isaacs, director of the Dialogue Project at MIT's Sloan School of Management, writes in *Dialogue and the Art of Thinking Together,* "As far as I know, no indigenous culture has yet been found that does not have the practice of sitting in a circle and talking."[1] The essence of Circles isn't new but tested over millennia and in many different cultures.

Aboriginal societies have preserved these spaces as a living part of their cultures, passing on ancient wisdom about how to call forth the best in us when we need it most. The willingness of aboriginal communities to share this nearly lost tradition with people from the very cultures that sought to assimilate or destroy them is a testament to the peacemaking wisdom that Circle principles instill.

The peacemaking Circle process described in this book does not, however, derive from any specific aboriginal tradition. Neither are its sources only ancient. Contemporary principles and practices of consensus-building, dialogue, and dispute resolution have helped shape our understanding of Circles. The process of Circles and our understanding of them evolved through the experiences of many communities that have used peacemaking Circles for crime. Circles are not, therefore, the latest technique or fad but an embodiment of both ancient and modern wisdom about how to keep human relationships alive, free, open, and constructive, especially when conflicts arise.

Today, we witness both the harm of disconnecting and the healing power of connecting. We need now, more than ever before, to find ways to connect with each other constructively, to understand and respect our differences, and to recognize the invaluable contribution each of us can make to creating community.

Circles provide spaces where this deeper connecting can happen—where conflicts become opportunities for building relationships. Circles offer families and communities forums for sharing responsibility for their well-being and for working through their differences to find common truth. Bringing people together in Circles is more demanding than resorting to force, power, or authority to balance competing interests; yet given the nature of the outcomes—mutual understanding, trust, and transformed attitudes, lives, and relationships—Circle work is far more rewarding. We continue to learn the power of Circles to support these deeply beneficial processes, and in this spirit, we share what we have learned from First Nation and other communities who use Circles to respond to crime.

Our proviso to readers. Because our sense of Circles grows from an ongoing exchange between ancient wisdom and modern experiences, we offer our reflections not as a final word but with an invitation to you to bring your wisdom and experience to what you read. If what we express resonates with what you know deep inside, then we encourage you to take it into your life. If it doesn't feel true to you, examine it and let it go. Though we write in declarative sentences, we intend everything in this book to serve as an invitation, not a directive. Our purpose in writing is to suggest possibilities for using Circles in dealing with crime and to support a wider participation in Circle work. We present what seems true to us at this moment; we don't know what is true for others or even ultimately what is true for ourselves.

Despite our passion for Circles, we're acutely aware that they're not panaceas. Circles are not appropriate for all conflicts. It's as important to understand the limitations of Circles as it is to understand their potential.

About terminology. We are following the convention used by many First Nations as well as other cultures of capitalizing a term that has special or sacred significance. Referring to the peacemaking process, the term "Circle" embodies many dimensions of meaning beyond the spatial or geometric, including sacred meanings, so we have chosen to capitalize it.

The term "First Nation People" refers to any aboriginal people whose culture existed before Western cultures arrived. The term has evolved to honor the primal sovereignty of these peoples and their cultures.

Using the term "offender" raises numerous issues, the main one being that it reduces a complex human being to only one aspect of the person's experience. To avoid stigmatizing someone who is working hard to change, many Circles have developed different terms: e.g., "applicant" and "core member." While sharing these sensitivities, we have nonetheless used the term "offender," simply because it identifies the person's place in the Circle process. In actual Circle practice, however, most communities refer to all participants simply by their names, not by their titles or classifications.

The term "victim" raises similar concerns, because it presents one particular aspect of a person's experience as the whole of that person. Many who have suffered crimes dislike the term because it connotes helplessness, powerlessness, and passivity—not qualities or conditions that anyone desires or finds helpful in working through trauma. "Survivor" is often used as an alternative. Again, while honoring these concerns, we have used the term "victim" because it readily identifies the individual's place in the Circle process.

In the literature of management and conflict resolution, the term "dialogue" has been given special meaning, contrasting with the terms "debate" and "discussion." In debate and discussion, we try to persuade others to accept our views. The model is one of competition in which one view defeats others. Dialogue has a different aim and dynamics. The goal isn't for one side to win but for a wider understanding to emerge. Hence dialogue invites a shared journey which enriches everyone. As William Isaacs notes, a dialogue is "a conversation with a center, not sides." This center—what's held in focus—involves an expanded appreciation of ourselves and others, of each other's interests, and of our connectedness. Whereas debate and discussion can occur spontaneously, dialogue requires planning—preparing all parties to embark on a deeper quest. Circles are places for dialogue. When we use the term in this book, we refer to this distinct way of relating.

Because the concept of community is central to Circle processes, it warrants some definition as well. "Community" refers to a group of people who have a shared interest. This common interest may be geographically related but need not be. It can also be a shared faith, a common daily experience such as a school or workplace, a shared desire to resolve an event or crisis in a good way, or a shared vision.

Our views concerning the current justice system. Finally, because we champion the use of Circles, people often ask us about our views of the current justice system. We each have had significant experiences with it: Barry has spent much of his career as a judge. Kay has spent nearly a decade as the restorative justice planner for the Minnesota Department of Corrections. Born into the Carcross/Tagish First Nation, Mark has served as a mediator, Circle keeper, and Circle trainer in the justice system within his community and in other communities in Canada, the United States, and internationally.

Based on our experiences, we believe we will always need a formal justice system. It's a cornerstone of the democratic process and the only means of dealing with those who deny responsibility or who have become too dangerous to remain in our communities.

It is our hope that widening the use of Circles with the justice system will not only strengthen communities but also free the necessary resources to address the most serious threats to the well-being of our society and communities—e.g., environmental harm, corporate crime, predatory violence, structural injustice—threats which communities are not equipped to handle by themselves.

Kay Pranis, Barry Stuart, and Mark Wedge
St. Paul, Minnesota; Vancouver, British Columbia;
and Whitehorse, Yukon

Peacemaking Circles

"The Ugly Feather"
The Story of a Circle Process at Work

CIRCLES BRING US TOGETHER TO SHARE who we are beyond our appearances. They're places of listening—of hearing what it's like to be someone else. They're also places for being heard—for expressing what's on our minds and hearts and having others receive it deeply. Telling our stories in the safe space of Circles opens windows on each other's lives, giving us moments when we can witness the path another has walked as well as feel that others appreciate our own path. The life stories shared are naturally transforming. Speakers and listeners are touched and changed; so are their relationships. Circles don't "make" this happen; rather they provide a forum—imbued with a philosophy and format that reflects it—where profound change is highly likely to happen.

Perhaps the best way to introduce the Circle process, then, is to share a story. Because honoring confidentiality is an essential guideline of Circles, all names and identifying circumstances have been altered or omitted throughout the book, unless specific permission has been given otherwise. This is the story of "the ugly feather":

⌒

Slumped in his chair, legs stretched out, arms folded and head down, Jamie listened as the feather was passed around the Circle. People were talking about him or his crime. He heard anger, but mostly he heard people asking him in many different ways: Why? Why had he spent so many years lost to alcohol and crime? When was he going to change? What would it take for him to change? Did he not care about the people he hurt? He was now twenty-one; when was he going to grow up? When was he going to take responsibility for his life?

Amidst the questions and anger were comments reflecting on his past—about the good things he had done. Some spoke about how he dealt with Elders and young people and about what he could be. These comments surprised him. Those were the only times he looked up. A furtive glance at those who spoke kindly about him briefly altered his otherwise frozen posture, sending messages that he didn't care and perhaps wasn't even listening.

But Jamie was listening. He was nervous, very nervous. He knew the feather would soon be passed to him. Soon he would have to talk and answer many questions. In court, anger, hostility, and a silent resignation to the process enabled him to slip through without being involved. Not here.

The feather came to him. He held the feather, twirling it in his hands. He paused. "I don't know what to say. I'm here because I want to change. That's it."

He passed the feather to John with a desperate hope that John might answer all the questions. John, a respected Elder, had been talking with him for weeks, trying to help him prepare for the Circle. John was in the Circle to support him. Jamie thought John would help him now.

John held the feather but didn't speak. Jamie worried that John might pass the feather back to him. John reached into his pouch and pulled out another feather. This feather was hardly recognizable as an eagle feather. It was twisted and large gaps suggested strands were missing. It was bedraggled, unkempt, and obviously not cared for— not a sacred object. John held up the feather for everyone to see.

"This is a very ugly feather. I don't know when I've seen such an ugly feather. This feather reminds me of myself when I was running wild and crazy. I was missing many strands, it seemed. I was twisted up inside, full of booze and anger, full of not caring for anyone, not even for myself. I was an ugly feather with lots of gaps in my life. I

want everyone to see up close how ugly this feather really is, so I'm going to pass it around while I talk. Hold this feather for a while. Look at it, feel it, and see how ugly and uncared for it is."

As the feather passed around the Circle, John spoke about his youth and broken life.

"I wasn't going anywhere but bad. I needed help, but I didn't know it. I needed someone to care, but I didn't know that either. Then Agnes, an Elder, came into my life. Slowly, you know, she always greeted me with a smile and asked how I was doing. Sometimes she gave me presents of food. She asked me to her house for tea. We talked. At first, she just listened. I did most of the talking. Soon she had me meeting with other Elders. Then I got working with an Elder on a trap line. I was still drinking, but it seemed like a lot less. She kept me busy.

"Pete, her husband, died that fall. It hit her hard. She turned to me for help. I didn't know how to handle that. I tried. I spent time with her. I went hunting and fishing to bring her food. She counted on me. That made me try.

"Soon I was taking courses from Sue, her niece, at the school. They kept me at it even when I went to jail for drunken driving. It was the first time I was ever embarrassed to be in jail. I'd been there before—lots of times. This time was different. I worried about Agnes. Who would get her food? Who'd visit her? People did, but I worried about it.

"She was worried about me too. Agnes saw to it that lots of people visited me in jail. They even had a dinner for me when I got out. I had to miss the drunk party planned by some of us getting out of jail the same day.

"She kept me at it, because she cared and got me caring. Agnes filled my life with caring people. It happened slowly, but it happened."

By the time John finished the story of his youth, the old, ugly feather had been around the Circle. Jamie held it for a moment, stroked it, and passed it to John. Holding up the old feather, John said, *"Now, look how beautiful this old, ugly feather has become."*

The feather was different. Maybe not beautiful, but certainly not ugly. Everyone, as they held the feather and listened to John, had stroked it almost unconsciously, as most of us do when holding a feather.

Still holding up the feather, John said, "This feather is like me. Once I was ugly, mad, and twisted up by anger. There were big gaps in my life. Many important parts of living a good life were missing. Then Agnes and several others came into my life. They held me, cared for me, and changed me like this feather. That's what we all have to do with Jamie. If all of us touch him with caring hands, we can help him become like this feather. Everything is beautiful, is sacred. It takes caring to bring out beauty, to make someone realize they are sacred, and to make us realize they are sacred. So I'm asking all of us tonight to touch Jamie's life, to care for him, to bring out his beauty, his sacred spirit."

John spoke about how Jamie had come to him asking for help. They had spoken several times, shared a sweat, and told each other the stories of their lives. "I believe in this young man. I believe he is genuine about wanting to change. In our old ways, we give a feather to those we believe in, those we want to know the teachings."

John stood, called upon Jamie to stand up, and presented Jamie with the once-ugly feather. "Jamie, this feather is yours. It says to you we believe in you. As this feather has been changed into something beautiful by the caring hands of everyone in the Circle, so will you be touched by the caring hands of all the people in our community. By respecting yourself, you will respect those who touch your life with care. Respect this feather. Let it keep you aware of what you are and of how people care about you."

The healing power of connecting with others in community, the wisdom of those who have traveled hard roads, the transforming experience of listening and speaking with respect, and the little touches of care and love that make a big difference: these potentials are present in us and in our communities. People like Agnes, John, and Jamie live among us. Circles connect us in ways that help us find them in each other and bring to life the sacredness of people like Jamie.

Each Circle is different, and no one can predict what will happen in any given gathering. On one hand, Circles have no fixed formula. On the other hand, definite factors—inner and outer, unseen and seen—help to create their unique dynamics. The more a group comes to know and use Circles, the less obvious some of these factors become. They get woven into a community's way of being together, until they seem almost invisible—just second nature.

For those new to the process and seeking to use Circles to respond to crime, though, knowing these factors helps tap the full power of Circles to support healing and transformation. By understanding the Circle process enough to trust it, participants let the process work and don't try to force it. They learn to allow the Circle to respond to the unique needs of a situation, and no two are ever alike.

Circles are, therefore, paradoxical. They're both structured and open, ordered and spontaneous, framed and free, limited and unlimited. This book explores one side of this paradox. It's as if the structured, ordered, framed, and limited parameters of the Circle provide the springboard for participants to come together in ways that are open, spontaneous, freeing, and unlimited in possibilities. The latter experience is what each Circle discovers on its own. It can't be written down.

This book describes the elements of Circles—their structure, frame, format, and overall process. Based on our own experiences, we can sketch the factors that go into making the Circle process what it is, and we can describe how these factors serve to make each Circle whatever it needs to be for those involved as they enter a difficult conversation. We can describe a Circle's anatomy, but that's very different from the actual experience of being in Circle—of witnessing a Circle come alive to address pain, offer healing, and help birth transformation. No words can capture that.

Chapter One

Circles: A Paradigm Shift in How We Respond to Crime

> *It is clear that the way to heal society of its violence . . . and lack of love is to replace the pyramid of domination with the circle of equality and respect.*
>
> —MANITONQUAT
> Elder of the Assonet Band of the Wampanoag Nation

CIRCLES HAVE A UNIVERSAL, enduring quality, because they operate from a few fundamental premises about human beings and our human condition.

First, Circles build on the premise that every human being wants to be connected to others in a good way. We don't thrive in isolation. Although negative life experiences may repress our innate desires to reach out, we need each other, and on some level, we know it.

Second, Circles operate from the premise that everybody shares core values that indicate what connecting in a good way means. As we will discuss in chapter 2, people the world over and from every walk of life turn to the same basic values to guide them in building good relationships.

Third, Circles assume that being connected in a good way and acting from our values are not always easy to do, especially when conflicts arise. Our core values may lie buried beneath the pain of adverse life experiences, or they may be overshadowed by values imposed on us by other people or by the institutions and systems that influence our lives. We may come to believe that we can't afford to act from our values if we want to survive. As a result, we

9

may feel isolated, and we may despair of being able to connect positively with others.

Fourth, Circles presume that, given a safe space, we can re-discover our core values, and that as we do, we also uncover our deep-seated desire to be positively connected. By providing the kind of space that supports both of these processes, Circles enable us to reach out to each other, which is one of our deepest longings. In Circles, our minds and hearts open in ways that the dominant Western model of criminal justice discourages, and we find ourselves connecting on levels we didn't believe were likely or even possible for us to experience.

Four Basic Shifts

Guided by these premises, Circles are designed to help us access our common humanity and from this basis to forge a healing response to conflicts. In so doing, Circles present a radical shift in how we respond to hurts and create social order. Specifically, Circles invite a paradigm shift:

1. from coercion to healing;
2. from solely individual to individual *and* collective accountability;
3. from primary dependence on the state to greater self-reliance within the community; and
4. from justice as "getting even" to justice as "getting well."

1. From coercion to healing

How can we live together without harming each other? And what do we do when harms occur? To respond to these questions, the criminal justice system relies primarily on the threat of punishment to prevent harm and the execution of punishment to change harmful behavior. In other words, it uses a system of external controls to maintain social order. This method exerts "power over"—the power of state authority over individuals—to react to crime and to make society safe.

Circles, on the other hand, engage "power with"—the power of people and communities to connect positively, to confront harms, to address deeper causes, and to seek transformation. When harms occur, Circles seek harmony by exploring our potentials for healing and rebuilding relationships. To prevent future harms, Circles cultivate healthy relationships with self and others. From a Circle perspective, healthy relationships are the key to good conduct, hence to public safety.

This approach to creating safe communities nurtures health and wholeness in every direction, within and without. By striving to heal wounded and broken relationships, Circles foster interactions that allow individuals, families, and communities to thrive. As social order flows from a shared inner sense of well-being, external coercion and state-imposed punishment become less necessary. Circles promote safety, therefore, by promoting healing: addressing the pain that gives rise to hurtful or violent conduct.

Shifting the focus from coercive measures to healing raises different questions about how we respond to crime. Instead of asking, "What should the standard punishment for this crime be?" or, "Should incarceration be mandatory?" Circles ask:

- How can we move toward healing?
- What can be done to repair the immediate harm and to prevent further harm?
- What wounds and circumstances—past and present—prevent us from having healthy relationships, both with ourselves and with others?
- What steps can we take to understand these wounds and to aid healing?

When a Circle explores everyone's genuine interests, punishment is rarely relevant to what offenders need to rehabilitate and become accountable, what victims need to heal, or what communities need to grow stronger.

2. *From solely individual to individual and collective accountability*

A second fundamental shift that Circles make in responding to crime centers on the question, "Who is accountable?" The criminal justice system endeavors to make offenders accountable as individuals. Circles hold individuals accountable as well for the harms they cause, but they also explore the collective dimensions of accountability, and there are many to consider. For example, have we ignored how social, cultural, racial, and economic conditions give rise to crime? Are we tolerating patterns that isolate individuals and lead to destructive behavior? Do our attitudes in some way create tensions within communities or polarize people into opposing factions? In other words, are we functioning in our families and communities in ways that contribute to the imbalances, misunderstandings, and inequities that culminate in crime?

Operating from the assumption that all things are connected—that we live in an interdependent universe—Circles take a more collective approach to accountability. This approach doesn't deny individual responsibility but balances it with the responsibility held by the family, community, and society. Mindful of our profound interrelatedness, Circles craft a response to crime that says: We as a family or a community bear some responsibility for what happened, and so we have an obligation to help make things right, including helping those who caused harm to assume their responsibility. We are all in some sense accountable to each other.

Judge Stephen Point of British Columbia captured this sense of interrelatedness when he observed, "If something happens to someone, we have to fix not just the person but the Circle, for we are all the Circle. That is the mystery of it—the connections among all of us."

3. *From primary dependence on the state to greater self-reliance within the community*

A third fundamental shift that Circles make lessens our dependence on the state and increases our reliance on communities to deal with conflicts and crimes. In many respects, the state, through the justice system, deprives communities of their conflicts and hence of the mutual growth that can come from working through them together. The state takes over, leaving the community in the role of spectator. Not all but many crimes can be opportunities for uncovering the deeper causes of breakdown, for rallying local resources to correct them, and in the process, for developing vital, healthy relationships.

A crime indicates that a community's sense of mutual understanding and respect is disintegrating. If we don't explore the underlying reasons for this trend or work to turn it around by building positive connections, we miss a rich opportunity for constructive change and leave the community vulnerable to worse breakdowns.

Circles provide a space—perhaps the only space in most communities—for us to discuss shared values and expectations. Through Circles, we can respond to crime by building mutual understanding and doing the hard moral work that transforms people living or working together into a community. In the Circle space, professionals and lay people forge partnerships that produce much more than a sentence for the offender. A new way of life can emerge. When communities take the lead in resolving and preventing crime, they can be far more effective than the state in producing deep, lasting changes. At the very least, Circles forge partnerships that can both lessen dependence on the state for dealing with crime and increase the self-reliance that constitutes the social capital of communities.

4. From justice as "getting even" to justice as "getting well"

The three preceding shifts generate a fourth; namely, a shift in our concept of justice.

First, if Circles are less about coercion and more about healing, then the justice that the Circle process generates has less to do with imposing punishments and more to do with cultivating our human capacities to change. In Circles, we share who we are in order to begin our healing journeys together. We reveal our wounds, stories, and histories, as well as our potentials. The justice we experience, then, is less rule-and-law centered and more human centered. It's a person-oriented, soulful justice—a justice that we both give and receive by respecting each other, expressing care and concern, and working for mutual healing.

Second, if Circles seek not just individual accountability but individual *and* collective accountability, then the Circle process generates a very different experience of justice in which everyone shares responsibility for working through the difficulties that precede and follow crime.

Third, if Circles spur a shift from depending primarily on the state to greater community responsibility, then Circle justice is less about exercising top-down authority and more about finding mutual interests through an egalitarian exchange. It's less about power-over and more about power-with. To use spatial images, Circle justice is less vertical and more horizontal.

In other words, with Circles comes a fundamental shift in how we both understand and experience justice. The traditional judicial process establishes justice by imposing variations of "getting even." To do that, the process depends on state authority and its power to control individuals—to "get even" in ways one individual can't do to another. In this context, victims and their needs are irrelevant except to justify punishment.

The Circle process, by contrast, generates justice by "getting well." In such a context, victims and their needs are of primary concern, because they're the ones who have been harmed. Justice devoted to getting well depends on victim participation in order to understand the victim experience. It asks the victims what harm has been done as well as what can repair it and contribute to healing. Not only victims, though, but everyone affected is invited into the Circle's process. Circles call us to support each other in healing ourselves, our families, and our communities, so that the needs surrounding crime can be addressed on many levels. The concept and practice of justice shift dramatically.

MAKING THE SHIFT:
A QUICK SKETCH OF A CIRCLE APPROACH

These four fundamental shifts in focus that Circles offer—(1) from coercion to healing; (2) from solely individual to individual *and* collective accountability; (3) from primary dependence on the state to greater community self-reliance; and (4) from justice as "getting even" to justice as "getting well"—generate a fundamentally different response to crime. Instead of being strictly an offender-focused process, Circles are driven by all interests. The following case illustrates how this can work.

A community sought to use a Circle for Hank, a young man who had seriously assaulted a police officer named Jim. The police opposed the idea. The community and the police agreed to use a Circle to explore why they disagreed. When the Circle convened, the long history of strained relationships between the community and police surfaced. Tensions ran high as people exchanged accusations.

Some community members spoke of a time when the police

had a reputation for "beating us up behind the bar on a slow Saturday night." Then, the popular view was "to run from police, but, if caught, to get in the first punch." The police denied this practice not only in the past but especially in recent history. They related how difficult it was to police a hostile community.

In the midst of finger-pointing exchanges, one police officer shared why he had first joined the force. He spoke of his own life in the community as a young man. He wanted to give young people what he'd never had. Following his openness, Jim, the officer who had been assaulted, expressed similar reasons for becoming a policeman. He shared his troubled journey from seeking to help youth to perceiving them as the enemy. The frustration and sadness he expressed revealed a person in pain, reaching out for help.

Jim's courage to be open prompted others to share their stories, triggering a round of deeper sharing. The Circle shifted to exploring how to repair the relationships not only between Hank and Jim but also between the police and the entire community.

Ultimately everyone agreed to use a Circle to deal with the offense, and through it Hank and Jim gained a much better understanding of each other. Beyond the immediate crime, though, the Circle addressed the long-standing causes of tensions between police and the community. By working through these unresolved tensions, the Circle produced a better foundation for mutual respect and trust.

As this case illustrates, Circles are not about proving who the bad apples are and then removing them; rather, they're about bringing people together to better understand each other and to heal old wounds. They don't focus on finding quick, final "solutions" but on building long-term networks of support—networks in which we share responsibility for working through difficulties as they arise.

Given this emphasis on mutuality and shared responsibility, Circles are not about winning or losing but about resolving things in ways that include and respect everyone involved. Conflicts, accusations, and angry emotions often arise in Circles and must arise for the Circle to understand where people are. But Circles are not designed to be an adversarial process. Instead, the Circle structure and format create a space safe enough to work through difficult conversations constructively, no matter how polarized we may feel. Rather than placing us in roles that can heighten hostility and defensiveness, Circles clear the way for us to find common ground.

Moving beyond pain and hostilities takes courage, which Circles foster by drawing the whole person into the process—our feelings, perceptions, hopes, fears, needs, and ideas. People can express things in Circles that they're not permitted to say in courts. In Circles, we're not only allowed but called to be real—to speak from our hearts about how we understand ourselves and experience a situation. If we can't include the physical, emotional, mental, and spiritual dimensions of ourselves, we can't be fully open and so can't create outcomes that include all aspects of our reality.

Circles invite not a few but everyone to participate. Involving everyone is essential to achieving justice. The Circle process doesn't, therefore, rely on one person (a judge) to decide outcomes but engages all participants in making decisions. No one's perspective is dismissed, nor are anyone's needs and concerns minimized. When people take an active role in peacemaking dialogues, they feel heard and discover that their voices carry equal weight. As a result, they're more likely to support the outcome, and their varied contributions increase the chances of creating options and forming good, constructive connections.

The justice that Circles generate emerges through this process. How we're treated, how we participate, who's involved, the degree to which we have input, our role in shaping results, how we're heard: these factors give us a sense of whether or not we've experienced justice. Circles do produce innovative sentences and support deep transformation in individuals and communities; more than these outcomes, though, the Circle's deepest product is its process. By participating in the Circle process, we find and experience justice.

After a Circle, a community member described her experience of justice as being quite different from what she anticipated:

> I went in to see justice done. It didn't get done—not in the way I went in wanting it. But the funny thing is, though I came out without the jail sentence I went in wanting to be imposed, I left with a real feeling of justice having been done. It was not about the outcome but about how the outcome came about that makes me feel like justice happened in there. I really got my say heard, just like everyone else. One thing for sure, I feel I learned a lot about people, about my community. I started realizing I didn't know as much as I figured I knew. I now know more about them and feel more connected to them—more a part of my community. No one could have convinced me before that this is how I'd feel—no one.

Conflicts as Opportunities

Given these fundamental shifts in responding to crime and achieving justice, Circles take a very different view of conflict. In 1925, Mary Parker Follett, a pioneer in management and community development, wrote in *Constructive Conflict,* "As conflict—difference—is here in the world, as we cannot avoid it, we should, I think, use it. Instead of condemning it, we should set it to work for us. Why not?" The way we choose to resolve differences affects us, our families, and our communities. It can either bring us closer together or drive us farther apart. How we respond to conflict reflects who we are and determines how we contribute to all the communities that fill our lives.

Circles invite us to engage in conflicts differently from the default stances of either avoiding a fight or bracing for one. The energies tied up in conflicts can be destructive, but so can all energies if we don't know how to use them constructively. Circles assume that conflicts are not intrinsically destructive but can be opportunities for creating understanding, respect, and a better-founded connectedness among us.

Episcopalian clergywoman Caroline A. Westerhoff explores the positive energy in conflict in ways that reflect what happens in Circle dialogues. Circles invite us to accept and honor how different we are. In her view, having our differences honored is a fundamental need, and this need lies at the root of our conflicts. If we imagine that conflicts grow from our "God-given differences"—from who we are as "originals" and "indispensable" in our "different-ness"—then we can see conflicts as celebrating our uniqueness. By accepting another's different-ness, we free ourselves to be different too. Caroline Westerhoff writes:

> To be who we are—creators in the image of the Creator—
> we must be actively engaged in the setting free of every
> other person to be who she or he is intended: someone
> different from who we are, someone who will see the world
> from another perspective, someone who will not agree with
> us. Anything short of such liberation is suppressive and
> destructive and ultimately death producing. . . .
>   Conflict is not just inevitable, as we are prone to say
> wisely and with a sigh of resignation. Instead it is part
> of the divine plan, a gift. Disruption is integral to God's
> order. Conflict doesn't sometimes provide us with energy,
> insight, and new possibility as reluctant by-products;
> newness cannot come without conflict. It is not a price

to be paid and endured, but a condition to be sought and welcomed and nurtured. . . .

To manage conflict then would be to allow it, not to suppress it; to open our doors and windows to its fresh wind. Following this line of thought to its ultimate conclusion, violence and war become not conflict run amuck, conflict out of all bounds, but the final outcome of conflict quelled. *They result when we will not allow the other to be different, when we deny our life-giving dependence on the different one with all our might and means.* [Italics added][2]

Because differences are inevitable, and conflicts tend to happen around them, a Circle approach assumes that conflicts are a natural part of life. Whether they're good or bad, constructive or destructive, depends on how we respond to them. If we respond with a process that encourages us to be respectful, honest, open, and compassionate, conflicts can bring about personal growth, deepening our connection to others and helping us value our differences.

This view of conflict invites a more constructive response to crime. We could treat crime as an opportunity to engage the uniqueness of offenders in ways that help them, their families, and their communities develop their different-ness. We could use it as an opportunity to engage the uniqueness of victims in their journeys to recover their lives. And we could use crime to help communities respond to the differences within them in ways that strengthen instead of divide them.

In Circles, participants explore these more constructive responses to crime by asking: How can we help an offender transform his or her negative energy into positive energy? How can we help a victim transform suffering into meaning? Indeed, how can we engage all Circle members in "the patient pursuit of [personal] excellence," to use Caroline Westerhoff's words, in ways that "encourage the differences in our companions along the way"?

Responding to these questions isn't easy, since the conflicts surrounding crime are rarely simple. Crimes involve more than they appear to, as do their resolutions. To harvest the positive potential of these situations, conflicts must be respected. By investing time and care in working through differences and by addressing not just the offender's needs but also the victim's, the community's, and all those affected by the crime, Circles respect conflicts in all their complexities.

Using Circles with the Justice System: Some Examples

This respectful approach to conflicts is proving highly effective in responding to crime and dealing with all the needs that follow. Circles were first introduced to the criminal justice system in Canada as an alternative way of sentencing that involves all stakeholders in the decision. Though most community justice Circles began with this purpose, Circle organizers soon discovered that sentencing was a minor part of the larger process of journeying with victims and offenders—journeys that involved generating networks of support to sustain personal change and prevent more crime. For this reason, the term "sentencing Circles" gave way to the more inclusive term of "peacemaking Circles," reflecting the larger aim to bring peace by building communities.

Communities continue to use Circles to determine sentences or to decide the terms of accountability for offenders. However, there are many other uses of Circles with the justice system. These uses help families and communities take responsibility for mending broken relations and creating new lives. They also give criminal justice professionals a chance to work with victims and offenders in new ways.

In juvenile justice, for example, one of the most rapidly growing uses are transition Circles, which facilitate reentry into the
family, school, and community when a juvenile leaves a facility.
The Circle process typically begins several months before release
and may continue for a year beyond.

"Circles helped me when no other placements did," said high
school junior Priscilla. Physically and sexually abused for six years
from the age of five by an older half-brother, Priscilla became a
chronic offender, tough and addicted. From the age of twelve, she
spent most of her time in group homes and detention facilities,
and the state of Minnesota was running out of options for her.
Then AMICUS arranged a Circle for her. A Twin Cities-based
nonprofit, AMICUS works with juvenile and adult offenders
after release through programs that rely heavily on family and community involvement. Attended by Priscilla, her family, and her
counselors, this Circle and the ones following it changed her life.
"We were all crying by the end of the Circle, but we got everything out, and I think it helped all of us," Priscilla said of her first
Circle. "What I learned out of all this," she now says, "is that you
can change and don't have to be a bad person."[3] Similar transition Circles are being used with adult offenders, especially with
offenders returning to society after a long sentence. Again, these
Circle processes begin long before an offender is released.

Circles are increasingly being used inside juvenile facilities to
deal with internal conflicts. At Minnesota's Red Wing juvenile
correctional facility, a youth was forcibly removed from a cottage
while shouting racial epithets at fellow residents. He was taken
to a separate secure cottage for a period of time. The remaining
youths were angry about his hurtful words, and staff members
were concerned about how to bring him back to live with his
group after his disciplinary time. They used the Circle to work
through the issues with the group as a whole and defused a volatile situation.

In another juvenile correctional facility, several community members conduct a weekly Circle with the young men in the program. The Circle provides an accepting, nonjudgmental space for these youths to talk about their struggles or just to sit quietly and be with one another.

In southern Minnesota, Circles are being used to support chronic women offenders on probation. The Circles are not involved in sentencing but work with the women after sentencing. They usually involve four to six community members who meet weekly with the "core member" (the woman on probation). Between weekly meetings, Circle members call the core member to check in. The frequency of contacts and Circles may be reduced as the core member's life stabilizes. Volunteers in the project commit to working with the core member for a year.

Similar Circles of support have been used for sex offenders who are considered high risks for re-offending. The Circles both monitor the activities of offenders and help meet their fundamental needs by building into their lives positive relationships and healthy social activities.

In a Canadian adult male prison's specialized living unit, Circles are used for community building and conflict resolution based on restorative justice. Staff and inmates participated together in a peacemaking-Circle training to establish the Circle process as a foundation for their community.

Circles have also been used to support victims in cases where the offender was not caught. A neighborhood school principal asked the local community justice Circle whether they could help a mom whose sixteen-year-old son was murdered by an unknown assailant. Circle members held a support Circle for the mother, the mother's sister, and several of the victim's siblings. The family members expressed their grief and fears. The aunt, who had been the pillar of support for the rest of the family, was able to let down and cry for the first time.

Sometimes Circles are called to serve professionals who deal with crime on a daily basis. After a particularly wrenching child abuse trial, for example, Judge Leslie Metzen of South St. Paul, Minnesota, asked Sister Pat Thalhuber of the B.V.M. Restorative Justice Ministry to conduct a healing Circle. Judge Metzen offered the opportunity to the prosecutor, jurors, law enforcement, and court personnel, whom the judge referred to as the peripheral victims of crime. Nine people participated, including the judge, four jurors, a law clerk, a court reporter, the prosecutor, and the police officer who was among the first on the scene and who did the investigation. Those involved later expressed how profoundly healing the Circle experience had been for them in processing the trauma to which they had been exposed. "In this particular Circle," Sister Thalhuber observed, "people had an opportunity to understand more fully their feelings about this case and to discover how much it truly had impacted their lives, both personally and professionally."

Circles can also help high-risk populations work through disputes and thus prevent violence from erupting. Outside Boston, Massachusetts, a grassroots, multicultural, human and community development organization named Roca, Inc. ("rock" in Spanish) uses Circles to help the teenagers, homeless youth, and gang members who come to its center. These "conflict Circles" address the full range of conflicts that youths face, from fights between youths to tensions between youth and their parents to long-standing hostilities between gangs or among gang members. Sometimes these Circles are called spontaneously when a flare-up occurs between youths at the center. More often, though, Circles are carefully planned, so that everyone involved is prepared for the encounter. In dealing with gangs, for example, Circles require extensive preparation to build trust before coming together. This preparation pays off. At Roca Revere, gang members involved in long-standing conflicts now come together in Circles regularly, whether the animosity occurs between individuals or groups.

Conflict Circles often focus on transforming relationships. They help young people learn new patterns of relating, mostly through the process of forming agreements, such as agreeing not to insult each other or do other things to trigger conflict. Seldom one-time events, conflict Circles usually meet many times to deal with an issue.[4]

These applications of Circles to justice situations by no means limit their use. We have seen the process used to discuss the placement of halfway houses in neighborhoods, to support victims, to work through budgetary expenditures among justice agencies, to develop common goals between different groups, and to develop community plans to address the causes of steadily escalating criminal behaviors. These varied examples illustrate the responsiveness of Circles to the wide range of needs surrounding the justice system and the potential of Circles to help people in crisis work through hurt and change in constructive, healing ways.

CEREMONIES OF REINTEGRATION

In all of these uses—with offenders, victims, justice professionals, and communities—Circles are essentially ceremonies of reintegration. Because crime signifies some breakdown of relationships that leaves people isolated, Circles focus on forging connections—reintegrating what has come apart. Disconnecting offenders from their families and communities will often increase whatever danger they may be to others. Whether offenders go to jail or not, Circles endeavor to rebuild their connections with their family and communities as instrumental to changing their lives. Circles seek ways to heal bonds that have been broken as well as to create new bonds.

To do this, Circles look beyond immediate appearances. To turn a destructive situation into something constructive or to heal what has been broken, Circles open us to experiencing each other as being more than we appear. Crime involves pain, hurt, and trauma. If we stop there, though, we won't be able to transform the situation or move beyond it.

The Circle's capacity for reintegration draws its strength from our capacity to discern in each other, in situations, and in communities more facets than one act or event initially presents. In Circles, we see inside each other's hearts and lives. We hear, for example, personal stories that explain how a person feels or why a deed was done, and we see ways to heal hurts and prevent more pain. Circles reintegrate people and communities by discovering the "more" that resides in each of us and by using it to build new bonds.

Specifically, the Circle process recognizes that we are more than our acts. It is appropriate for a person to feel bad for harming others, but it's not appropriate for others to treat that person as a lesser or defective human being, lacking in worth or undeserving of respect. This distinction between the act and the actor opens the door to positive change, because it frees people to grow beyond the place of behaving hurtfully. Accordingly, Circles call on offenders to take responsibility for what they did, to gain a full understanding of the harm caused by their behavior, to make reparation, and to seek personal changes to prevent further offenses. Circles support this transformative process, so that those who have acted hurtfully can choose a different course, access their potentials to connect positively, and be reintegrated into their families and communities.

Victims, as well, are more than what has happened to them. All the gifts, talents, strengths, dignity, and personal resources that they possessed before the crime are still theirs. However, victims have definite needs as a result of the crime—physical, emotional, mental, and spiritual—that must be met. Circles acknowledge the harm to victims, validate their pain and suffering, affirm that what happened was wrong, and attend to victims' needs and interests. In these ways, Circles help victims access their capacities to deal with trauma. By participating in Circles, victims often feel less isolated by the pain caused by the crime and are gradually able to reintegrate with their families and communities.

Circles also break down barriers between professionals and the community, allowing the community to see the professionals as more than "just a badge." Professionals reintegrate with their communities beyond their roles. James Roche, a street team worker for Roca, reflected on the first time he sat next to a policeman in a Circle:

> It was funny, because the first day [in Circle], I think I sat next to a cop. I didn't realize it until the feather went around, and I looked to my right, and I said, "Oh wait! Oh, this is the first time in my life I'm sitting next to a police officer." It was hard, but it was worth it to hear some of the coppers, what they say. At the same time, they listened to us. And I finally seen something there . . . like I could see, this could work. Just off that Circle alone, to this day, I say, this could work.[5]

Communities, too, are more than lives juxtaposed by external factors—geography, work, or institutions. They have their own unseen life force, which we can either nurture or let languish. Circles create spaces to discover the potential of any community to be a force for good in people's lives. At Roca, for example, Circles have demonstrated people's potential to "show up for one another." The ceremony of coming together in a respectful process has a reintegrating effect, inspiring people to pull together in ways they otherwise wouldn't do:

> The Circle brings people together to focus on what they have in common, what they most want for themselves, their family, and their community, and how they can work together toward these goals. It is a profoundly hopeful process. When James [Roche] organized a Circle within the community to support a young man going through a difficult crisis, he and others in the Circle realized that it was one of the first times that the community had come out to be there for each other in a positive and supportive way. That, in and of itself, was a powerfully moving experience for the community to just see their capacity to show up for one another.[6]

By encouraging us to access the "more" that we are on all these levels, Circles help us move toward a healthy balance of personal power after an experience of either powerlessness or inappropriate power over others. If we've felt powerless, Circles help us regain our capacities to be autonomous and to speak our truth. If we've exercised inappropriate power over others, Circles help us access our capacities to witness the hurt we've caused, to feel remorse, and to develop respect. Because we express our sense of power through our relationships, we change power imbalances by working them out with others. It's not something we can achieve alone. Circles provide the means to do this—to rebalance the flow of power in our relationships. As ceremonies designed to reintegrate us, Circles help us reweave the fabric of our families and communities, so that we're held in a good, power-balanced way.

In short, Circles offer a dramatically different response to crime from the current justice system. By bringing people together to address profound human needs, they help us reach out to each other and discover deeper connections—connections that for some have rarely, if ever, graced their lives. In our experience, the possibilities that follow for healing and transformation—for weaving our lives anew—can exceed our hopes and imaginings.

Courts and Circles: A Comparison

	Courts	Circles
Participation	Restricted: primarily reliant on experts	Inclusive: primarily reliant on community
Decision-making	Adversarial	Consensus
Issues	Broken state laws	Broken relationships
Focus	• Past conduct • Individual responsibility • State legal requirements	• Past, present, and future conduct • Individual and collective responsibility • Needs of all parties
Tools	• Banishment • Punishment • Coercion	• Reintegration • Healing/support • Trust/understanding
Procedure	Fixed rules	Flexible guidelines
Results	Winners/losers	Finding common ground to maximize all interests

Courts aspire to settle disputes. Circles aspire to resolve differences by improving relationships, by addressing underlying causes, and by enhancing individual and community self-reliance.

Chapter Two

The Inner Frame of Circles

We are all related, and we are all related in a good way.
—MARK LaPOINTE, METIS, CIRCLE KEEPER

PEACEMAKING CIRCLES HELP US resolve conflicts in a good way, one that honors the needs and concerns of everyone involved. To do this, especially in criminal justice situations, Circles need to create a safe space. What does safety mean, though, and how do Circles create it?

Safety flows from the frame, format, process, and participatory nature of Circles

To feel safe, we need to feel protected—that who we are will not be dismissed, dishonored, or attacked—not only physically but also emotionally. Put positively, we need to feel that we will be valued as a person and that what we share will be respected, whether we're confused or clear, upset or struggling, angry or silent. We want to be treated as much as possible from our wholeness.

Circles respond to the need for safety by establishing a frame within which dialogue can proceed. Many factors contribute to the security of the Circle space. We're grouping some of the most basic elements into two broad categories: the inner frame and the outer frame of Circles. In this chapter, we will explore the inner frame, including the core values, principles, and some of the philosophy underlying Circles. In the next chapter, we will explore the Circle's outer frame—the more visible elements; namely, the keepers, the talking piece, the guidelines, the ceremonies, and the consensus-based decision-making. Together, the inner and outer

31

frames establish a container for safety; they hold a safe space for dialogue without being authoritarian or controlling.

In chapters 4 and 5, we will explore how the inner and outer frames converge to create the general Circle format and the larger Circle process for dealing with crime. These include many additional features that build safety into each step—e.g., preparing everyone, keeping them informed, listening to where people are, not pushing them into situations for which they're not ready, and finding out from them what they need to feel safe.

Besides these basic components of Circles, yet another source of safety comes from the fact that participants are involved in setting up the frame for dialogue. The Circle's structure and process are not imposed wholesale but are themselves shaped by dialogue and consent. Consensus-based decision-making applies not only to *what* Circles decide but also to *how* they go about deciding it. Involving everyone in forming key elements of a Circle's dynamics generates a safe space, because then people commit to sticking to the process as best they can. Consensus agreements about values and guidelines provide a baseline of safety.

For example, if we have listened to others talk about the values they need to have honored in order to feel safe, if we've expressed the values we see as vital, and if together we've agreed to follow a core set, then we have a better idea of what to expect from each other. From this foundation, we know everyone will do their best to practice these values in dealing with the issues at hand. If we or they stumble, we know the rest of the Circle will work to restore a safe atmosphere. We commit to helping each other maintain a safe space.

In other words, Circles are a careful, measured process, and ultimately the total process makes them safe. Because Circles hold everyone in their wholeness, many participants experience the space as also sacred, enabling us to interact from our best selves. Not only the Circle's structure but also the process of arriving at it generate these qualities of safety and sacredness. We're able to move forward in having a difficult conversation with assurances that the experience will be constructive.

Choosing Peacemaking Values

Circles transform conflicts into opportunities by applying ancient wisdom about human relationships. This wisdom begins with appreciating the role that values have in human conduct. Values are our compass in life. The values we bring to a situation determine how we respond. Before dealing with any conflict, therefore, we need to clarify our values. What values can help us work through our differences in the best way possible?

Core values that are universal

In our experiences of introducing peacemaking Circles around the world, we have found that people from every culture, walk of life, and religious perspective identify the same core values to guide their interactions. When asked, inmates and judges, children and Elders, people in rural towns and metropolitan areas all name similar values to guide their conduct. The description or emphasis may be different, and the list may vary in length or terms used, but the type of value is always the same: positive, constructive, healing values—values supportive of the best in ourselves and others. People don't generally say, for example, "I'd like to be as arrogant, judgmental, and vindictive as I can be in working through this conflict."

Because people have their own experiences around values, though, the same value can carry many implications. We have found that each group must explore their values together, so that they arrive at a common understanding of what the people involved mean by each one. People from two different cultures, for example, might express respect, courage, or love in different and perhaps opposite ways.

Exploring people's experiences around values plays a vital role in bringing a Circle together. It forms an essential starting point and one that can occupy considerable time, even extending over multiple sessions. Such questions as, "What is real courage?" or, "What do honesty and trust require?" have no pat answers, yet how we understand these values affects how we act on them. At Roca, wrestling with values and the guidelines that follow from them (which we will discuss in chapter 3) is an ongoing process:

> It is not unusual for a Circle with young people to spend hours and even days discussing [values and] guidelines. In the first series of Circles, Saroeum [Phoung] kept [a Circle] for thirty young people at YouthStar, and the group spent two whole days, four to six hours each day, just talking about guidelines. At Roca Revere, in the talking Circles with gang members, the guidelines discussion will focus on particular values: What does respect mean to you? What does love mean? What does confidentiality mean? The guidelines involve a genuine discussion about the meaning of these words and the concrete implications of living those values. This may be the first time young people are asked: What does it mean to feel "respected"? What does it mean to "love" someone?[7]

We have selected ten values—those most frequently named by participants as essential: respect, honesty, trust, humility, sharing, inclusivity, empathy, courage, forgiveness, and love—to illustrate how they can operate in Circles dealing with criminal justice cases.

Respect. Johnny Johns, an Elder of the Carcross/Tagish First Nation, said, "Respect is the main thing. If you don't have that, you don't have anything." A Minnesota public defender said the same: "In a Circle, respect comes first. We may not always agree, but we must always have respect." Respect means honoring ourselves by acting in accord with our values, honoring others by recognizing their right to be different, and treating others with dignity. We express respect not only in how we speak and act but also through our emotions and body language. Respect comes from a deep inner place of acknowledging the worth inherent in every aspect of creation. According to many First Nation teachings, "All the races and tribes in the world are like the different colored flowers of one meadow. All are beautiful. As children of the Creator, they must all be respected."[8]

In Circles dealing with crime, having respect means seeing past both the offense and the offender to discover a person's humanity. Being respectful doesn't mean that we ignore the offense or refrain from holding the offender accountable. It means acting with respect for all the flowers of the meadow, all the children of the Creator.

Honesty. When we give and receive respect, we find it easier to be honest, both with others and with ourselves. Honesty starts with self-honesty—owning our thoughts, feelings, and actions. We lower our masks and let ourselves be as we truly are. Instead of dissembling to protect an agenda, we share our inner world and begin a dialogue aimed not at defending our perspective but at openly questioning it to discover a wider truth.

Being honest can be powerfully transforming, as one offender discovered. Joe had been through the system many times and viewed the entire process as a game. He approached the Circle the same way, hoping he could tell his old lies and get away with it. Joe had rarely been honest with himself or anyone else. He had never questioned either his own perspective or his rationalizations for his criminal behavior. In the courtroom, his contributions, expressed mostly through counsel, were "made up and dressed up to gain an edge in the game."

During the Circle, when the counsel passed the talking piece to Joe, he handed it on with little more than a grunt. But the honesty and courage of others to speak their truths broke through his defenses. When he finally spoke, Joe discovered the power of his own honesty: "I did not believe what came out of me. I never had talked in court before. [In the Circle,] I did not expect the reaction, either in me or in them." His honesty was cleansing as well as liberating, and it became the basis for a very different relationship with his community. Many years later and crime-free, he believes that "honesty [gave me] a new life. It saved me."

Trust. With respect and honesty comes trust. Whether or not we agree with others, we learn to trust that we can work things out in a good way by acting in accord with our values. Trust begins with ourselves: trusting who we are and that we can follow through on what our values call us to do. Trust challenges us to take risks, first in exposing who we are and then in reaching out to others. These risks are not foolish, though, because Circles are devoted to creating a foundation for trust. The result is that trust creates more trust. In a Circle that brought together juveniles and law enforcement personnel, for example, a police officer took a risk by sharing his fears and dreams with gang members. In turn, his courage to reach out moved a gang member to do the same, revealing the humanity of both.

Humility. Valuing someone's uniqueness can be a powerful gift to another, and humility enables us to do this. With humility, we honor another's voice by holding a listening, receptive posture. As we do, we experience who a person is in an open, nonjudgmental way. We take in his or her way of seeing the world, which expands our own perspective.

Humility also grows from recognizing our own limitations. We don't know what may be true for others or what their experiences may be. We can easily make mistakes in our assessments of people and situations. Because our view is limited, we need the input of others to have a more complete understanding. Humility calls us to focus more on discovering the wider truth than on advancing our own needs.

By opening us to the innate worth of others and reminding us of our limitations, humility fosters our growth and connects us more meaningfully to our immediate and larger communities. We open ourselves to what different people have to offer. Professionals in the justice system, for instance, do much better personally and professionally when they acknowledge their limitations as well as appreciate and encourage the contributions that others, especially community members, can make. One prosecutor who initially opposed Circles because he dismissed community input came to regard it as invaluable. "For me," he observed, "the most important moment was recognizing that the community had more important things to contribute than I did or ever could have. The law part is important, but not as much as I believed."

Sharing. Sharing is about opening ourselves to others and allowing our relationships with them to develop as they will. For this to happen, we need to release the urge to control people and situations. Sharing calls us to shift our stance from angling for control to recognizing the interests of others. Then real sharing starts. We discover how interdependent we are, as we explore the larger issues contributing to a conflict.

Sharing with others leads to a shift in power, which develops through a two-way dynamic: yielding power on one side allows others to take power as they assume responsibility. The focus ceases to be on who has control. Instead, open sharing lets power and responsibility flow naturally to those in the best position to exercise them. Barry's experience as a judge in Circles illustrates this dynamic:

> In the early sentencing Circles (now called peacemak-
> ing Circles), participants addressed their presentations
> to me as the judge. They felt a need to convince me of
> the outcome. When it became clear that all of us would
> decide the outcome—that a consensus would govern
> the sentence and that I could not rely on my powers as
> a judge—several things happened. They took on more
> responsibility, and I was accepted as an equal voice, which
> also meant I became fair game for teasing and being ig-
> nored. The focus of the conversation changed. Before, the
> community felt they needed to challenge me as a repre-
> sentative of the justice system over the sentence, arguing
> that jail "did nothing good." They believed (with justi-
> fication) that justice officials regard jail as the primary
> sentencing tool.
>
> Moreover, as long as the discussion focused on
> whether or not the offender would go to jail, the bad
> aspects of the crime and the offender were underplayed,
> while the offender's good points were overplayed. People
> couldn't get beyond discussing the offender's fate, which
> left the victim's interests unaddressed.
>
> Once they realized that control over the outcome was
> to be shared equally, they dropped the debating stance, and
> we began to explore how to address everyone's interests.
> Sharing power among equals generated a dialogue that
> elicited a more open and truthful exchange. The victim's
> experience and needs were no longer secondary. The Circle
> began to ask different questions concerning what to do not
> only about the offender and the victim but also about the
> underlying problems that gave rise to the crime.

The power that we professionals have arises from both our skills and the institutional roles we play. When we participate in Circles in ways that share this power, we send a compelling message about inclusivity, equality, and respect for others. However, sharing our decision-making power may not include sharing ourselves—who we are personally. Because professionals live in a world that imposes expectations of "professionalism" and "objectivity," we face unique challenges in sharing our personal hopes, fears, and stories. Yet these deeper levels of sharing are precisely those that bring the greatest transformation.

Inclusivity. Inclusivity means actively seeking to involve everyone whose interests are affected. In the spirit of inclusivity, we respect others' contributions and strive to incorporate their concerns into the outcomes, even if laws or circumstances don't require it. Inclusivity reflects the holistic character of Circles, and it inspires a generosity of spirit that draws everyone in instead of keeping some out. Edwin Markham, the late-nineteenth to early-twentieth century "poet of democracy," expressed the power of inclusivity in a well-known quatrain:

> He drew a circle that shut me out—
> Heretic, rebel, a thing to flout.
> But love and I had the wit to win:
> We drew a circle that took him in.

The following case illustrates the power of this value for building community. In the early stages of starting a Circle process, one community was inclined to exclude a police officer whose negative views about community justice were well known. Moreover, one of the Circle organizers had personally suffered a bad experience with the officer. The group was on the verge of deciding not to ask him to be on their organizing committee, when one member reminded the others of the importance of inclusivity. A dialogue about this value followed that ultimately led to inviting the police officer to join them. Years later when the police officer had become an ardent advocate for community justice within the police force, the initial decision that almost excluded him became a standing joke and ready reminder of inclusivity and its valuable effects.

Inclusivity also applies to how offenders are treated. When a Circle decides an offender requires time in jail for healing and accountability, that person isn't excluded from the community. The community will take steps to look after the family and the affairs of the offender, to visit the offender in prison, and to prepare to reintegrate the offender into the community. When a Yukon Circle sent an offender to jail as part of a consensus plan, an Elder observed:

> How you send people away from our community is how
> they will come back. Send them away in anger, they come
> back angry; send them away with love, they come back
> with love in their hearts.

Including everyone creates an atmosphere of tolerance and respect that's essential for a healthy community.

Empathy. Henry Wadsworth Longfellow wrote, "If we could read the secret history of our enemies, we should find in each man's life sorrow and suffering enough to disarm all hostility." Understanding each other through our stories reduces the distances separating us and inspires compassion. As we learn more about the paths each of us has walked, the urge to judge others falls away, and we find meaning in giving and receiving empathy.

Whereas pity can feel condescending, empathy expresses the equality between ourselves and those who suffer. It recognizes and shares the suffering that goes with our common journey through life, and this empathetic awareness can bring a profound shift.

For example, in so many Circles, offenders, on hearing the stories of victims, are filled with an empathy that inspires remorse and sweeps away the rationalizations they once used to excuse their criminal behavior. Similarly, victims, on hearing the stories of offenders, can sometimes begin to move away from their anger. Some find themselves experiencing empathy for a person whose abuse-filled life led to his or her abuse of others.

Courage. Holding values and living them are two different things. We can see farther than where our feet fall. That is, we can desire to live more consistently with our values than we often find ourselves able to do. There are no easy formulas—no single "right" way of living our values. We need courage to find our own paths and to grant others the space to do the same, especially when we or they stumble.

Bert, for example, was one of the first success stories of a community's peacemaking Circle project. The community was as proud as he was of his accomplishments. He had dramatically changed a lifestyle that had amassed over thirty convictions, and he remained substance-free and crime-free for more than six years. Then he re-offended with a serious crime. He let the community down, and everyone was shaken. In jail, Bert summoned the courage to reconnect with the community, and they found the courage to respond.

In the year since his jail sentence ended, Bert has, on his own initiative, completed a difficult treatment program that no one previously thought he needed. He knows the course that his values offer, and he has rediscovered the courage and the support to regain a path based on values. The community has accepted him again, recognizing that life's journeys have no end, only many turns as well as times of being lost.

Courage doesn't mean the absence of fear but the ability to acknowledge fears and to go forward in spite of them. Courage carries us beyond fear and apathy. It enables us to move past the worst, whether in ourselves, others, our private lives, or our work environments. For Bert and his community, courage was necessary for both to start again.

Forgiveness. These values—respect, honesty, trust, humility, sharing, inclusivity, empathy, and courage—bring us to a place where forgiveness becomes possible. Forgiveness emerges from the dynamics of each individual's healing journey, which generally begins with learning to forgive ourselves. Yet even here, forgiveness can be a complex process. It's not something we decide to do as much as something we move toward or find ourselves growing into. No one should be told to forgive someone else or be expected to do so. Forgiveness involves a much deeper experience of finding inner peace along paths unique to each person.

Granted, if self-hatred or self-recrimination linger, these self-rejecting energies often block our way to wisdom, love, and peace. Circles help us see the good that lies within ourselves through the mirror of others' open, nonjudgmental listening. As we learn to honor our positive aspects, we move towards forgiving ourselves for whatever we've done. In his review Circle a year after starting the process, one offender reflected:

> You may not understand this, but my anger, my crimes
> come as much from hating myself as from hating others.
> I've done bad things. I hate myself for that. In the past
> Circles, you've made it possible for me to stop hating
> myself and to begin forgiving myself. I'm not there, but
> I'm going in that direction. I can feel it. What's made this
> possible is your helping me see what is not bad in me—
> giving me the support to move beyond my anger for what
> happened to me in the past and to stop hating myself for
> what I've done.

When we're able to move toward forgiveness, the pain of suffering loosens its grip on our lives. Forgiving someone who has caused us harm can profoundly shift the dynamics of a relationship, at least on our side. It also changes our relationship to life, not just to the one who hurt us. Forgiveness releases the heavy negative energies that anger and resentment produce and opens space for light and hope to flow in. We experience life differently, as if a heavy cloud has lifted and joy can return.

Kathy, an older woman and the victim of a break-in, was particularly traumatized because the crime happened as her husband was dying of cancer. A year later, she found herself still absorbed in anger and fear regarding the young man, who was now coming to the end of his jail sentence. She requested a healing Circle with the offender. In the Circle space, she was able to express her pain, receive support from the community, and experience the offender as a young man who had made a mistake. Seeing him as "another human soul trying to put sense into life," she was able to take a big step forward in her journey of forgiveness. In subsequent months, she felt lighter, more hopeful, and able to access her natural joy and optimism. She reengaged in the positive activities she had dropped, and her life blossomed again. Of her experience in Circle, she writes:

> By the end of the evening, this offender of nightmare, fear, and much anxiety looked like the fellow who sat beside him—another human soul trying to put sense into life. I see that person as myself in many ways, that frightened, sometimes beaten soul who is trying to get back upon life's horse and ride into the beautiful sunrise of life.[9]

Forgiveness doesn't wipe out the fact or memory of the crime, neither does it remove the necessity to redress a crime's causes. It does, though, enhance our capacity to strive for inner peace.

With forgiveness, we avoid the self-destructive effects of anger and hatred. Though it's naturally easier to forgive someone who is contrite, forgiveness isn't an exchange but a gift to others and ourselves. We can act on our values, including forgiveness, whatever someone else may do.

Love. Most of us aren't comfortable expressing love in our public lives and especially in our conflicts. Yet we need love to develop our connection with everyone and everything. Love deepens our awareness that we're not separate, however much we may appear to be. All the values contribute to our ability to love, while love in turn expands our ability to embrace other values. We may not be able to sustain whole, unconditional love, but as we work with our values, our capacity to love expands. As it does, love becomes a healing force in our lives.

Love's healing power can be felt not only in close personal relationships but also in communities and in criminal justice work. For example, twenty years ago, four youths were directed to be sentenced by a Circle of Elders, their first case. It wasn't going well. The Elders spoke of their fears and of the shame they felt that young people from their community were harming others. The youths sat sullenly defiant. They claimed that they had nothing to do in town and that no one cared. The exchanges deteriorated, until it appeared that nothing more could be done. Their cases would have to be sent back to court.

Then Dora Wedge, a respected First Nation Elder, began to speak of love. She wanted to find a way to work through her fear and anger and to connect in a loving way with these young men. "You know in the old days, that was the way it was. The young people were loved, protected. They too loved, protected, and helped look after old people like us. They kept our homes supplied with water, wood, and food. We told them our stories. I—all of us here—we do love you." Her expression of love hung in the air. It begged for a response. One young man broke the silence: "You don't love us. You talk about us in bad ways to others. You ignore us. You never invite us to do nothing."

An animated exchange followed for almost two hours. They talked—really talked. For the first time, they began to work through negative assumptions, misunderstandings, and frustrations. They talked about many things: about changes needed in the community, about changes in their relationships, and about their own hopes and fears. The evening ended with promises to "say 'Hi' when we meet," to "spend some time doing things we both like doing," to figure out how to bring Elders and youth together more in a good way "like it was" and to "talk again soon."

When the youths left, one of the Elders exclaimed, "Hey, we forgot to give 'em all a sentence!" They had imposed a much better sentence than anything a court might have done. The youths had apologized for disrespecting their community and their Elders by committing crimes. The Elders had accepted responsibility for "thinking and talking in a bad way" about them and for "not teaching youth more through our stories."

Their cases were not sent back to court. One youth died a few years later. The rest, unlike their peers and unlike their previous histories, were never again in any serious trouble with the law. On their own initiative, the youths looked for ways to quietly help the Elders. They put sawdust on the Elder's pathways in winter, dropped off fish in summer, and gathered berries for them in spring. One youth began a very different path that years later led to his selection by the Elders and his community to be Chief. The Circle process had dramatic results, yet the process began to work only after Dora Wedge had the courage to talk about love and to explore its peacemaking power.

These ten core values are interdependent and reinforce one another. Together, they enhance our capacity to delve into the sources of conflict and to develop solutions that maximize all interests. Though we may not be able to practice all our values fully, we nonetheless need them to guide us. We continually clarify our values not to admonish ourselves for failing to act on them adequately, but to help us make choices that reflect how we most want to be. Saroeum Phoung, a core member of the leadership team at Roca, reflects on his struggle to live "Circle values":

> Once you learn Circle values, you can't just go back. . . .
> Well, you can go back, but we always catch ourselves—
> "I'm not being in a good way, so now I'm gonna have to
> go back and apologize, 'cause I was such an ass." Before
> we learned Circle, we could be such asses, and we were
> like, "Alright it's cool," 'cause we didn't know any better.[10]

But it's not all on us as individuals to make the shift to living more mindfully aligned with our values. The space of the Circle itself helps us learn how to act in more value-consistent ways. Kay had an experience that made her see the difference in her own behavior in and out of Circle:

> I was asked to help resolve a long-term hostile work
> environment among clerical staff in a prison. Sue Stacy,
> Nancy McCreight, and I were working with the staff to
> see if they would be involved in a Circle. There was a
> tremendous amount of distrust among them. We met in
> small groups with individuals to talk about participating.
> In one-on-one conversations with a hesitant participant,
> I got anxious when she expressed reservations about being
> in the Circle, and then I tried to persuade her, think-
> ing that it wouldn't work if everybody wasn't there. She

chose not to participate. In the Circle later that day, other participants expressed their concerns about her absence. In the actual space of the Circle, I felt no anxiety about her absence and was able to accept that she needed to do what was right for her. After that Circle, I looked back on the day and realized how differently I held myself in those two spaces—when I was trying to persuade her and when I sat in respectful acceptance of her choice. I saw how different those two energies were for me. I realized that the space of Circle helped me to act in harmony with my values.

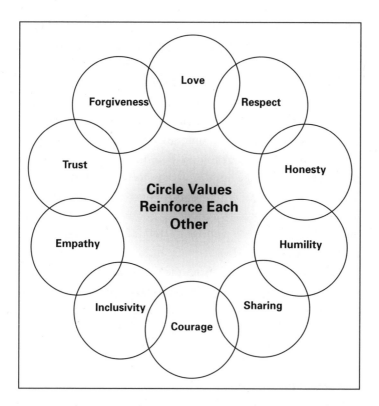

Personal values versus conflict norms

Peacemaking values form the lifeblood of healthy families and communities. The outer forms of our relatedness may change, since we as individuals change. But as long as we follow these values as we connect with each other, we find meaning and support from our relatedness. Conflicts move relationships into deep transitions, and in the midst of change, no one knows the outcome. If we rely on our values to work through our differences, our relationships often improve, though they may change. Indeed, it's when conflicts arise that we need our core values the most.

Each person's list of values may expand or be expressed differently. Whatever our values, though, we don't want conflict or stress to draw us away from them. Otherwise, we can lose ourselves pursuing whatever it takes to win, sacrificing our integrity and self-respect in the process. Hurtful strategies are familiar enough: judging, blaming, and accusing others; being deceptive, manipulative, resentful, hostile, insensitive, arrogant, belligerent, aggressive, emotionally cold, unforgiving, or grudge bearing. Reactive to the dynamics of competition, these generally accepted norms of conflict make our interactions feel highly unsafe.

We find ourselves deviating from our core values, though, not because we want to but because we don't know how to bring our best values to conflicts. Instead, following the models we've observed in others and in our institutions, we make an automatic, unconscious switch from the values we aspire to following to those we believe are necessary to hold our own in conflict. Switching to a combative set, we become people we don't recognize or want to be. The fighting values take over, and before we know it, even if we "win," loving relationships that we had for years are lost.

The following story is sadly a common one. After a long, expensive, and emotionally charged civil litigation, John, who won his suit against Fred, expressed deep regret. Fred had been a lifelong friend and business partner. In the court process, John believed they both had been driven to distort the truth and exploit their respective weaknesses. Their relationship of many years was finished. So, too, were all the relationships between John's and Fred's families and among their friends who were pressured to choose sides. For John, the money won now seemed far less significant than the loss of relationships. Most important, John regretted what the experience did to him: it drew out "the worst parts of my character." He believed the adversarial nature of the process had compromised many of his values. He didn't like who he had become.

The ancient wisdom informing Circles suggests that the values we use to build good relationships are precisely those we need to use in conflicts. When we bring our core values to our difficult conversations, conflicts become opportunities to let our relationships change and grow stronger, whatever the outcome may be. Acting on our values does not mean giving up or surrendering but rather addressing our conflicts in a different way.

Through their frame, process, and sacred space, Circles make it easier for us to stay aligned with our core values, especially in emotionally intense situations. The values are not about how to *do* a Circle but how to *be* in Circle. In the Circle space, we observe how others act on their values, and this inspires us. As we listen deeply and speak from the heart, Circle values move us beyond positional thinking and professional roles and call forth the best in us. We find the courage to follow a deep but often suppressed instinct: to reach out to others. To deal with crime in our communities, we need—more than any number of new justice resources—the means to do this: to reach out to others in a good way.

BUILDING ON PRINCIPLES: PUTTING VALUES INTO PRACTICE IN SETTING UP CIRCLES

How, then, do we create these means? How do we put our values into practice in forming a Circle, which involves a collective endeavor? How can we construct a Circle process that both meets the unique needs of a situation and does it in a value-based way?

These questions come up every time the need for a Circle arises. Perhaps someone has suffered a crime but doesn't want to press charges because the offender is a friend, neighbor, or relative. How does that person (or his or her supporters) convene a Circle to deal with the situation in a peacemaking way? Or perhaps a case has gone to court, and either the victim, the offender, or their supporters want to call a Circle to resolve issues that court processes are not designed to address: how do they proceed? On a larger scale, how does a community go about instituting an ongoing Circle project in the neighborhood to provide an alternative process for offenders, victims, and communities? Faced with these needs for a Circle, organizers confront a further question: Do we need a Circle process for ourselves as we develop the Circle process for the situation?

To respond to these questions, we have identified thirteen guiding principles for drawing a Circle together, whether it's for a specific situation, for a more enduring community Circle project, or for the internal workings of an organizing committee. These principles serve as foundation stones. A Circle process built on them holds individuals equally in a good way, because they help us stay aligned with our values as we work through difficult issues together.

We have found these principles useful precisely because every Circle is unique. Circles work best when they're molded to fit the distinct needs and circumstances of a community and a case.

There are no rigid formulas for designing or running them. Yet organizers consistently turn to these principles as a starting point for crafting a Circle process, because they have a good track record for creating a successful Circle space—one that supports participants in acting from their values. The principles provide reliable reference points as communities or groups form and implement a Circle process.

Specifically, the principles offer guidance on questions that people involved with starting a Circle—big or small—invariably find themselves asking:

- What guides our conduct in Circles? Every social process—from a football game to a court procedure to a job or wedding—carries a corresponding way of behaving that's appropriate. What is it for a Circle?
- How do we determine who should be there or at least invited to attend? What interests are at stake, and how can they be involved?
- What criteria do we use as we handle the logistics of gathering a Circle together?
- How does the Circle treat participants? What treatment can we promise a person who is considering whether or not to attend?
- If we feel someone should be there but he or she isn't inclined, is it appropriate to try to pressure that person into attending?
- Should people—young and old, victims and offenders— be allowed to speak for themselves, or should we arrange for others to speak for them, as happens in court?
- What overall purpose are we seeking, since this vision guides us in designing the components?
- Who should be involved in designing the Circle process?

- Is it necessary to stick to our original Circle plan, or is it more effective to adjust the Circle process as we go along?
- Should we try to limit Circle dialogue to issues pertaining directly to an event, task, or project, or is it better to invite an open sharing?
- What is the relationship of the Circle to each participant and to the larger environment?
- Is it necessary for people to leave their spirituality outside the Circle or be silent about it, as is necessary in other public processes?
- What reasonable expectations can we have of each other as fellow Circle participants, both during and after Circle gatherings?

These issues arise as we seek to come together in a different way. Essentially, they boil down to these questions: How do we go about constructing a Circle process that has structural integrity? And if we put together a sound Circle process, how do we maintain that integrity as things change? It's easy to get lost in the complexities of difficult cases or be swayed by powerful personalities. Since Circle methods require time and effort, we may also be tempted to take shortcuts for expediency. Plus, old habits of responding to conflicts may creep in.

When we face such challenges, Circle principles serve as checks, keeping us true to the core values and steering us away from the slippery slope of ends justifying means. According to Circle wisdom and experience, means and ends reflect each other. "We can't get to a good place in a bad way—ever." For Molly Baldwin, executive director of Roca, this statement has become a mantra, reminding her that the same values and methods used to build a process will be used to run the process—and the values that people experience as an outcome. Rev. Martin Luther King, Jr., said: "One day we must come to see that peace is not merely a distant goal that we seek, but a means by which we arrive at that goal. We must pursue peaceful ends through peaceful means."

Circle principles serve to keep our means and ends congruent. As issues arise, they help us answer the question: What is a good, Circle-consistent way to handle this? Organizing a community Circle process assumes a significant responsibility that involves other people's lives and happiness as well as our own. These principles support organizers, giving us confidence about how we can stay on a good path as we birth and tend our journey with Circles. Designing and running Circles according to them, we can engage a Circle's full powers.

The principles may, of course, be described in various ways, and other principles may apply that we haven't included. We have derived these principles from the experiences of many communities in starting and running Circles as well as from successful consensus-building practices.[11] Most of all, we have identified principles that translate our shared values into the practice of Circles.

1. Circles call us to act on our personal values

What guides our conduct in Circles? The "first principle" encourages participants to bring their values to every phase of the work, from designing a Circle process to engaging in the Circle itself. The principle is simple, but its effect is profound: Circles change how communities deal with crime by first changing how participants deal with each other.

Acting on our core values is, as we've said, an ideal and aspiration, and we continually learn how we might act from our values more fully. This is why attending to our own personal growth through self-examination, self-reflection, and inner questioning is essential to Circle work. The structural integrity of Circles depends

on our capacities to bring our personal values to the process. To do
this, we need to regularly check our thoughts, decisions, and conduct against our values.

One community, anxious to begin using Circles after some
had attended a Circle training, met for several months to start a
community Circle initiative to deal with crime. As the months
passed, though, differences among participants grew, bickering
increased, and attendance dropped. Conflicts within the group
about how to use Circles drained everyone's enthusiasm for the
project. After many months of these meetings, not one Circle had
been held. *Roberts' Rules of Order,* not the Circle, had been used to
deal with the differences.

Hearing about this experience underscored for us the importance of this first principle; namely, that we need to bring our
Circle values to each facet of our work with Circles. The values we
use to build and manage a Circle process unavoidably permeate its
use. It's not possible to build a process with one set of values and
run it with another.

For this reason, initiating and then sustaining a community
Circle process become far easier when most, if not all, participants
have attended a Circle training, which explores personal values ex-
tensively. Then, when problems arise, as they invariably do, those
with Circle training turn more readily to their personal values for
guidance and are less likely to lapse into the more conventional,
adversarial modes of response.

2. *Circles include all interests*

How do we determine who should be invited to participate in the
Circle? Whose interests are at stake, and how should these people
be involved? Everyone affected by a crime has a moral right to participate in designing and using a Circle that will make decisions
about it. To this end, Circle organizers make appropriate infor-

mation readily available, so that everyone can choose whether or not they need to be involved. The broader the participation, the greater the Circle's potential to develop a wide base of support and produce innovative, community-sensitive solutions.

Further, the more diverse the perspectives represented in Circles, the more balanced and comprehensive the outcomes can be. Circles make space for every point of view, since this is how Circles protect themselves from becoming one-sided. Those directly affected by a crime are kept informed and their participation is sought. Indeed, organizers work to engage all segments of society. They make an extra effort to involve those who may oppose Circles, extending standing invitations.

In one community, for example, the victim advocacy groups initially opposed Circles. The Circle committee proceeded without them but continued to invite them and keep them informed. Each Circle meeting sought to respect the interests of the victim advocacy groups, even though they weren't present. In time, these groups did become involved and supportive. One community organizer commented, "I think we both learned a lot in walking the long road to working together."

3. Circles are easily accessible to all

What criteria do we follow in handling the logistics? Circles must be simple to use in every respect; their process must be "transparent" for everyone. Participation shouldn't be limited by a certain level of knowledge, skill, money, connections, or resources. Accordingly, this principle encourages us to identify barriers to participation and remove them. Setting times that make it easy for everyone to attend, picking central meeting places, helping with transportation, baby-sitting, and expenses if necessary: demonstrating these practical concerns recognizes the importance of everyone's involvement. Care expressed about such simple things can make a big difference in drawing in all those who want or need to attend.

The judicial system, by contrast, isn't "transparent," clear, or easy to use for many. Legal language is technical and not designed to be understood by lay people. Complex procedures discourage people from representing themselves as either victims or offenders, and yet hiring and working with a lawyer can be daunting. The net effect is that the judicial system isn't "easily accessible to all." Circles are a people's process, and this principle reminds organizers to go the distance in making it easy for people to get involved, no matter who they are or what their circumstances may be.

4. *Circles offer everyone an equal opportunity to participate*

Are some people in a Circle more important than others, and do their words carry more weight? Circles are radically democratic: each person has an equal voice and role in decision-making. No person's perspective is more or less valued than another's, regardless of age, race, gender, personal history, or position. Each view needs to be heard, because each person has insights, feelings, and experiences that lend balance to the Circle. By demonstrating in practice that each participant gets an equal voice, Circles affirm each person's worth and value.

Naturally, personal involvement may vary according to interest, but it should not vary according to status, position, ability, or means. In *The Millionth Circle,* Jean Shinoda Bolen writes, "A Circle is non-hierarchical—this is what equality is like. This is how a culture behaves when it listens and learns from everyone in it." The more participants feel that they have full opportunities to participate and that their contributions count in decision-making, the more they experience the process as being fair, and consequently, the more they're likely to support the outcome.

Creating an equal opportunity to participate begins with being sensitive to what may cause someone to feel less than equal. Making people feel welcome and comfortable in a strange setting send important first messages about equality. "It was the first time they came to Roca. We made sure they felt welcomed," an organizer said. Providing equal access to information, considering all perspectives thoughtfully, including all views in summaries, and then factoring all interests into any final decisions: these practices demonstrate the principle of equality in Circles.

5. *Involvement in Circles is voluntary*

Should anyone be pressured to either attend or speak? No. No one should be in a Circle who doesn't want to be present or who feels obligated or expected to participate, neither should anyone feel pressured to talk. Much of the power of Circles stems from this principle, because it affirms participants' ability to choose for themselves. Making choices empowers us.

When a community shares a Circle training, the justice personnel and people from different parts of the community who attend are far more inclined to participate voluntarily. One justice official noted, "In training over those four days, we got to learn not just about Circles but also about each other. Now I know these people. I trust 'em enough to call 'em up when I have a problem. It makes it easier for me to work with them."

Granted, for offenders, participation in Circles isn't entirely voluntary. The choice for them is often between going to Circle and having a voice in decisions, or going to court and having no voice. They choose the Circle process as "the lesser of two evils," and in the agreements they make with the Circle, their attendance is mandatory. Nonetheless, the element of choice is there, because they can always elect to return to court. Derek, for example, made the latter choice after he got fed up with community members trying to help him change his life. He'd grown up on the streets and wasn't in the habit of answering to anyone, so he elected to return to the court process. The whole Circle showed up for his court sentencing, some in tears. The court sentenced Derek to prison, but he later reapplied to the Circle when he came out, re-offended, and faced new charges. He then chose a path that involved working with the community.

The voluntary nature of Circles is a source of strength, not weakness. The strength flows from the responsibility that participants share to keep everyone involved. Everyone must be mindful of more than their own interests, otherwise others leave, since they're free to do so. The choice to remain in a voluntary process communicates a strong message about commitment within a community.

6. In Circles, everyone participates directly as themselves

Should people be allowed to speak for themselves, or should we arrange for others to speak for them, as in court? In Circles, people speak for themselves. We're more likely to take responsibility for agreements if we've had a voice in making them. When we speak our truth directly, we're more able to own what we say and do. Direct participation heightens everyone's involvement. Dennis Maloney, who engages offenders, victims, professionals, and community members directly in peacemaking processes, observed, "Participation trumps prescription every day."

This principle does not imply that anyone *must* speak. Participants can always pass the talking piece in silence. Yet for those unaccustomed to speaking in public, the slower, reflective nature of the Circle space, the support of other participants, and especially the talking piece create an environment that often brings out quiet voices. This happened to the mother of a juvenile when the talking piece (a feather in this case) came to her:

Well, I'm not one for speaking in public—never have been—so I was real surprised to find myself talking so easily and so much inside that Circle. When the feather came by that second time, I just started, seeing others do it. All that they said made it easier for me. It was good for me and him [her son] that I did speak, I feel that for sure.

Offenders in particular are more likely to own what they did when they participate directly. As they confront their actions before those affected as well as those who care about them, they experience a deeper sense of accountability. Very often, their sense of themselves and their relation to their community shift dramatically as a result.

For example, Vichey Phoung, a Cambodian refugee who became an ardent gang member, is now a street worker in Roca's VIA (Vision, Intent, and Action) Project. During his time with the gang when he was also coming to Roca, Vichey was charged and convicted of assault with a dangerous weapon and sentenced to time in prison, which he served. "In addition to the formal justice process, Vichey agreed to be accountable to himself and his community through a Circle process. Before the sentencing hearing, Vichey participated in a series of Circles in order to address the harm he had caused to others and to himself."[12] Vichey described the impact the Circles had on him:

I had a Circle myself before I went to jail. Circle didn't lessen my time or help my case. I was meeting with the Circle just on my own, and that is the Circle I really didn't want to be in very much, 'cause it was so hard— you yourself acknowledging the harm, what you've done and the need to talk about it, who I've harmed, what ripple effect it had. To be able to be in conversation about

that stuff, then to understand and be aware: you yourself
hold yourself accountable.[13]

When the talking piece came to Vichey, he reflected:

> You know, I went to jail for what I had done. I done some
> pretty serious stuff. And when I got to jail, I was the only
> person there who knew why I was there. I went to court.
> I didn't talk; the lawyers talked, the judge sentenced
> me, and I went to jail. And everybody in jail was either
> innocent or "wrong place, wrong time." Nobody really
> owned what they did. I know what I did. I knew why I
> was there.[14]

Vichey summed up the impact of his direct participation in
the Circle: "I think Circle helped me become who I am today."[15]

7. Circles are guided by a shared vision

What is the overall purpose of the Circle process? Although each
Circle is uniquely adapted for a situation, an overriding shared
vision guides a community's use of Circles. Shared visions are
like living organisms, weaving individual efforts into a coherent,
focused endeavor. A motto of the Fire Flower Centre for Nonviolence and Conflict Management states: "If there is only one
person dreaming, it remains a dream. If many people are dreaming
together, a new way will be created."

The strength of a shared vision depends on how we create and
sustain it. If we develop it through consensus and sustain it that
way, we're more likely to experience our shared vision as a force
that unites us and directs our community. This may seem obvious—what is "shared" if not that?—and yet it's easy to assume that

a group already shares a vision and hence not bother to clarify it. Taking the time to explore a vision together pays off in many ways, from focusing our energies to deepening our sense of meaning in what we're doing. Revisiting the vision annually, for example, can renew everyone's commitment to a common purpose.

The shared vision naturally evolves as new participants join and as the Circle committee gains experience. Because shared visions can be powerful motivators, one way to build them is, again, for Circle participants to share a Circle training. These trainings are not information downloads for the uninitiated; they're experiences of being in Circle and working together to find a deeply held common ground.

8. Circles are designed by those who use them

Who should design the Circle process—e.g., what types of Circles might be needed and how might they link together—especially as the situation unfolds? Because Circles are participant driven, each community designs its own process for each case. Using the values, principles, and shared vision as constant guides amid change, organizers can be far more flexible in designing Circles than if the process were stamped from a preset mold. They continually adapt the process to the shifting needs and circumstances facing the community.

Indeed, the designing activity never ends. When new people join a community Circle committee, their fresh insights contribute to the designing work as much as do the accumulated lessons of more seasoned members. Engaging people in constructing Circles deepens relationships and inspires a shared commitment to making the process work. It instills pride of ownership. And it inspires a resolve to treat failures as lessons and to persist in making the Circle process serve the community successfully.

9. Circles are flexible in accommodating unique needs and interests

Is there one set way of doing a Circle process? And if we map it out one way, can we change it? As we've said, Circles are open and flexible. They're responsive to the situation at hand, since their content and focus are never fixed. Being flexible sends the message that individual needs and interests are more important than following rigid procedures.

The same flexibility applies to designing and running Circle processes, especially as the case unfolds. Naturally, some of the designing is done up front, such as sketching a basic direction and mapping initial steps. But as new needs emerge and more issues come to light, organizers must feel free to respond to what's happening.

To honor the uniqueness of a situation, organizers learn to adapt the process to fit the conflict, rather than the reverse. If we try to make the conflict conform to a predetermined process, we may overlook some special circumstances and so fail to respect certain needs. Being rigid about the design diminishes the Circle's capacity to use crime as an opportunity for making positive changes—e.g., for developing community connections or generating innovative solutions. By contrast, the more responsive the design of Circles is to a specific case—what kinds of Circles are needed for whom, when, how often, and for what purpose—the more effective the total process can be.

10. Circles take a holistic approach

Should we try to limit Circle dialogue to issues pertaining directly to an event, task, or project, or is it better to invite an open and wide-ranging sharing? Circles operate holistically to respond to crime in transformative ways, and many of these principles reflect their holistic nature. Most obviously, the principle of inclusivity expresses the need to include all interests in order to find workable, healing solutions. But the holistic approach is expressed in other ways as well.

First, because Circles strive for a holistic sense of what happened, they don't confine the dialogue to the immediate issues or circumstances. Honoring the connectedness of all things, they operate from an awareness that events don't happen in isolation. When a crime takes place, it occurs within a context comprised of many factors. All these factors warrant a place in Circle dialogues.

Second, Circles track problems to their roots to understand the deeper causes of crime. They focus community energies not only on mending the immediate harm but also on preventing future crimes. By pursuing systemic causes, Circles work to change the conditions that create crime and keep it going.

Third, Circles draw on the power of connectedness not only to address causes but also to find solutions. Accordingly, Circle processes are most effective when they engage all aspects of the community. In Yukon, whenever Circles involved a broad spectrum of community leaders—religious, educational, judicial, social service, and business—the process achieved solutions that otherwise seemed impossible. Without broad-based participation, community volunteers often become overwhelmed with the demands of pursuing a holistic approach. Crime not only has its roots in all facets of a community; it finds its healing there too.

Fourth, Circles also take a holistic approach by drawing on our whole being: physical, mental, emotional, and spiritual. No aspect of who we are is excluded, since conflicts affect us as a whole person. Our hearts race, our feelings grow intense, and our thoughts fly in many directions while we seek to regain our connectedness. As a result, each aspect of who we are has something to say about how to forge a balanced process and outcome. In many Circles, solving the immediate conflict becomes secondary to telling our

stories—talking about ourselves, our journeys, and our relationships. Sharing who we are connects us on deeper levels, and this
helps us move past feeling stuck in intractable differences.

Fifth, to allow dialogue to move to deeper levels, Circles invite
participants to express their emotions—not accusingly but with
respect—as part of the process. Crimes are highly charged experiences. Ignoring the emotional component hinders our ability
to address deep-seated differences and to begin healing. Because
Circles keep the dialogue respectful and reflective even in highly
emotional situations, Circles are spaces where the energies in our
emotions can be released and processed with others. As this happens, even the most painful energies can start flowing in constructive directions.

In other words, a Circle's approach is holistic, because it attempts to embrace all interests, address crime's underlying causes,
rally the resources necessary to find lasting solutions, and engage
the whole person, including our emotions, in change. This may
sound like too much to ask of one process, yet given the nature of
Circles and how they're structured, it's natural for them to function in all these ways.

11. Circles maintain respect for all

What is the relationship of the Circle to each participant and to the
external environment? Everything about the way a Circle operates
needs to convey respect for the participants. Respect permeates
the Circle process, from how its gatherings hold everyone in an
equally good way to how they maintain a respectful relationship
with the wider community.

For example, nothing in Circles should convey a message of
ranking, regardless of a person's history or circumstances. Ranking
communicates respect for some but disrespect for others. It also
imposes filters that narrow our capacity to hear what another is

expressing. In *The Other Way to Listen,* a children's book written by Byrd Baylor and illustrated by Peter Parnall, an Elder teaches a young person to listen to nature and the earth. At one point, he says, "Take a horned toad, for example. If you think you're better than a horned toad, you'll never hear its voice—even if you sit there in the sun forever." The equality pervading Circles enables us to respect others and hence to hear in a deep way what they're saying.

12. Circles invite spiritual presence

Is it necessary for people to leave their spirituality outside of the Circle or be silent about it as in other public processes? Again, being holistic in nature, Circles invite all dimensions of who we are into the dialogue, not only in Circles dealing with crime but in all Circles. Engaging our wholeness opens us to a spiritual sense of each other. As we share what's inside us, we work through pain, despair, fear, joy, and hope together. We connect with deeper places in ourselves and others, tell our soul's stories, and thereby unlock capacities to understand, heal, change, and love that are profound.

In his book *Ethics for the New Millennium,* His Holiness the Dalai Lama defines spirituality as "concerned with those qualities of the human spirit—such as love and compassion, patience, tolerance, forgiveness, contentment, a sense of responsibility, a sense of harmony—which bring happiness to both self and others."[16] He continues, "Spiritual practice according to this description involves, on the one hand, acting out of concern for others' well-being. On the other, it entails transforming ourselves so that we become more readily disposed to do so."[17] In this sense, Circles are a form of spiritual practice, which further explains why many participants experience their space as sacred. In Circles, we walk the sacred ground of the values we hold most dear, and we use those values to transform ourselves, so we can make peace with others and work for our common well-being.

Based on soulful sharing, the spirituality in Circles respects different religious beliefs but doesn't impose a religious view. Connecting from the heart and embracing our shared human condition are without denomination. They remind us of the sacredness of each person and of our mutual endeavor to come together in a good way, especially when it seems hardest to do. Going into our hearts, we're able to bring down walls, release burdens, and access our best selves in ways that bring us closer together. One Circle participant experienced a sense of being "one with each other":

> It was something else. I've never experienced that before and really haven't since, not that strong. But when we were all feeling her pain and her daughter's pain, we were in pain. It was the closest moment I've ever had to feeling like family to strangers. You could say everyone in that Circle began to be one with each other. Some people in there I didn't know before, but for a while there, I knew them—knew they all walked on the same trail and would continue on the same trail as me in a way. We were different, very different, but very related to each other. I'm gonna talk about that Circle feeling forever.

Such moments of spiritual connecting can alter our course dramatically. It's not uncommon in Circles for people to make unexpected shifts, as they reconnect with themselves, their values, and each other. This can happen for any participant, not just key players. "You go there to help the victim or the offender," Minnesota judge Gary Schurrer observed, "but you end up helping yourself the most." No matter what the issue, as we venture into the root of conflicts, we experience what it means to open our hearts, give voice to our souls, be present with others, heal strained and broken relationships, and through it all, to call forth our spiritual capacities to change.

13. Circles foster accountability to others and to the process

Whether or not we experience a sense of spiritual connectedness, what can we reasonably expect of each other both during and after Circle gatherings? Being a consensual process from the start, Circles make everyone more accountable. Yet the nature of accountability that Circles inspire is very different from the kind that comes from court experiences. While courts try to coerce accountability principally through punitive sanctions and professional interventions, Circles inspire accountability through value-based actions and connections formed within the Circle. When we share the pain and joy of Circle dialogues, we feel a strong need to honor these new connections by keeping the agreements. Accountability on all sides grows from the joint effort to make positive change.

Guides for community building

These thirteen principles serve as *guides,* not rigid rules. Respecting them includes questioning how best to apply them to each Circle process. Though the principles carry equal weight and reinforce each other, in some circumstances, certain principles may require extra attention. Together, they frame how we create constructive spaces for responding to crime—spaces where personal accountability, healing, caring, spirituality, love, compassion, and forgiveness develop naturally.

Using these principles to design and run peacemaking Circles also cultivates community-building skills. The principles inspire the vision and hope we need to maintain healthy, active communities.

They also help us pull together to assume responsibility for crime and to do the hard moral work of being a community. For those involved in designing and running a Circle process, the committee's own Circles provide continual opportunities for building respect, trust, understanding, and a working experience of community.

THE WORLDVIEW UNDERLYING CIRCLES: MEDICINE WHEEL GUIDANCE IN SEEKING BALANCE AND WHOLENESS

The circle: A metaphor for a worldview of wholeness

Circles, both their traditional, indigenous practices and their current adaptations to dealing with crime, build on an underlying worldview—one that sees the universe as characterized by wholeness, unity, and connectedness. The values and principles we've explored offer different ways of expressing this view of the cosmos, bringing the philosophy down to informing how we view ourselves and interact with others. We treat each other in respectful and ultimately sacred ways, because we see each person as part of the whole and indispensable to it. We also see ourselves as connected to all other beings, and so what happens to them affects us too. Our connectedness gives us the responsibility to care for each other and to help mend the webs that hold us.

The circle shape itself is a universal metaphor for this worldview. If we ponder the circle image, various features besides wholeness, connectedness, and unity come to mind. For example, all parts of a circle are equal, since every point on the circle is in exactly the same relation to the center. As a metaphor, a circle does not suggest hierarchy—it has no top or bottom. Also, each aspect is connected with and hence inseparable from every other. No part can be cut out and thrown away without violating the quality of the circle as a whole. A circle also conveys balance—that each aspect is held in a balanced relationship with the whole. If the circle were lopsided, it wouldn't be a circle anymore.

Set in motion, a circle symbolizes cycles—patterns of moving forth from and then returning to the origin. In a practical way, a circle metaphor assures us that things will come around again; we'll always have another chance to correct mistakes and to do things better, as long as we're open to learning and trying again. In a larger sense, the circle suggests a way of understanding life processes; namely, that life moves in rhythms and cycles. As we understand the cycles of life, we're able to move with them more mindfully.

Mark, a member of the Carcross/Tagish First Nation in Yukon, shares his personal sense of this philosophy—how it's rooted in the "Circle of Life" and how it informs his culture:

> Circles are modeled after natural cycles within the universe. Communities have always used some form of Circles, and many still use Circles within their daily lives. As a child, I remember my mother speaking of the relationship all people have with the Land. She talked about how we moved with the Land and creation, and that all things move in a circle. She talked about the rounds of life and how we moved with the animals. We spent the spring near the rivers for fish and beaver, then moved to the lakes and marshes for the berries and lake fish, and then to the mountains to harvest the larger animals and put up food for the winter, then the valleys for the furbearing animals. This she referred to as the rounds of life, that all people make the rounds of life. Our life goes from entrance into this world from the spirit world through the stages of life until we return to the spirit world. This is known as the Circle of Life.
>
> In our creation mythology, our stories reflect how life

is set in motion by circular patterns, how the sun, moon, and universe are circles; the campfire in the snow establishes a circle; when we drop a stone in the water, the ripples make circles. Just like the potlatches when we give gifts and throw away our differences and difficulties, our problems disappear like the ripples in the water.

The Medicine Wheel: holding differences in balance within a whole

Over millennia, many First Nation People have walked the wisdom embedded in this philosophy, which their traditions teach through the "Medicine Wheel," or "Sacred Hoop." Represented by a circle marked off in quadrants by the four directions, the Medicine Wheel is "an ancient and powerful symbol of the Universe"[18] and functions as a sacred teaching for many North and South American First Nation People.

Through the quadrants, the Medicine Wheel shows how diversity and unity come together in balance. Each quadrant symbolizes a different aspect of life, stage of development, or set of qualities. Yet all quadrants are needed for the circle to be complete. Unity doesn't mean sameness; it means balancing differences that are each valuable to the whole. No aspect is more or less important than another, and each deserves its rightful place in our lives.

We are physical, mental, emotional, and spiritual beings

As a symbol, the Medicine Wheel represents many profound levels of meaning. For the purposes of this book, we'll focus on one facet of its teaching; namely, its holistic view of human beings. From a Medicine Wheel perspective, we're not only matter or only mind, neither are we only our emotions or even only spiritual beings. We are all these together—physical, mental, emotional, and spiritual. All four facets are essential to our existence, and they must be balanced for an activity to be successful or for a person, family, or community to be healthy.

Whenever one aspect outweighs the others, imbalances occur. People or communities get sick, languish, or behave hurtfully. According to the Medicine Wheel's teaching, the road to health for both individuals and communities lies with focusing on the missing aspects and expressing them more fully.

This teaching has much to offer how we respond to crime. Courts, for example, are almost exclusively mental processes with physical consequences (fines or incarceration). They exclude emotional and spiritual expressions. As a result, courts are limited in the balance they're able to achieve. Indeed, their lopsidedness causes imbalances. Emotions are not healed, nor are people or relationships made whole.

Viewed holistically, crime isn't about broken laws but about broken lives. Crime shatters our sense of wholeness, and we don't know how to put ourselves, our lives, or our relationships back together. During his time on the bench, Barry struggled with the inability of the courts to address the emotional needs of everyone affected by crime, including court professionals:

> As a judge, I listened to the suffering, isolation, and injustices that both led people to commit crimes and that their crimes caused in the lives of others. I understood and then accepted that the need to be impartial required that neither I nor other professionals show the pain and anger we felt. So I did not shout with rage or release the tears welling up from deep within me. While my emotional restraint honored court practices, it dishonored the stories of the people whose lives marched through the court—a march that allowed neither their wounded spirits nor their painful emotions to be addressed.

Like many judges and other professionals in the court process, our restraint comes at a price—a price we realize long after our families and friends recognize it. Our restraint either hardens our hearts or rips into our capacity to joyously embrace life, or both. I screamed in rage on wilderness walks and broke into tears at nothing at all or at seemingly innocuous events. When deep emotions are shut down, they do not disappear. They emerge in other forms in many parts of our lives. I believed there had to be a more respectful, more holistic way to embrace all the aspects of crime—aspects that the court shuts out.

Drawing on all four dimensions to bring balance

Circles strive to do this—to address the full dimensions of who we are as we deal with crime in our lives and communities. In most cases, hearing everyone's story is an essential starting point. Because our stories often draw in all aspects of our being, telling them supports healing and generates a sense of justice. We delve into the physical, mental, emotional, and spiritual impact of crime on us, which moves us toward a more balanced awareness of what happened, where we are now, and what the next steps might be.

Besides sharing our stories, Circles offer other ways of bringing into balance all aspects of our being as we work through painful experiences. Specifically, the very experience of being in Circle draws on all four aspects:

- *Physically,* we honor the Circle with our physical presence: we "show up" and stay mindful that how we use our bodies can communicate messages to others. Arriving late or walking in and out, for example, can convey disrespect. We stay physically present through all the difficult conversations. At the same time, every-

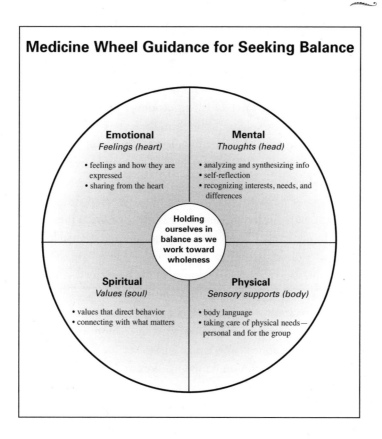

Medicine Wheel Guidance for Seeking Balance

Emotional
Feelings (heart)

- feelings and how they are expressed
- sharing from the heart

Mental
Thoughts (head)

- analyzing and synthesizing info
- self-reflection
- recognizing interests, needs, and differences

Holding ourselves in balance as we work toward wholeness

Spiritual
Values (soul)

- values that direct behavior
- connecting with what matters

Physical
Sensory supports (body)

- body language
- taking care of physical needs— personal and for the group

one in the Circle attends to taking care of physical needs, from needing Kleenex to taking breaks. Several communities have used music, dance, art, and other activities to engage participants, so that they can connect in ways that include physical expression.

- *Mentally,* we bring our minds' total capacities to the Circle. When others are speaking, we try not to let our thoughts wander. We put our full mental energies into listening to whoever has the talking piece, keeping an open mind, and focusing on our values to help form our

responses. We also use our minds' abilities to analyze a
situation, to process and synthesize information about
it, and to generate new paths forward. To do this, we
exercise two other important mental skills. First, we
maintain high levels of self-reflection, paying attention
to our own thoughts, feelings, and reactions during the
dialogue. Second, we remain alert to identifying interests, needs, and differences, both within ourselves and
among others.

- *Emotionally,* we speak from the heart. We stay present with our feelings and express ourselves from these
  deeper levels. Circles are not forums for intellectual lec-
  tures or debates. They're places for soul searching and
  expressing our deepest feelings in the best way we can,
  which includes sharing needs, hurts, and fears.

- *Spiritually,* we open ourselves to the opportunities that
  Circles present for experiencing deeper, more authentic
  levels of connectedness. Sharing stories, for example,
  reveals our common humanity. We also feel connected
  when others articulate what we feel but haven't yet put
  into words. As we explore values together, we sense that
  we're more alike than different and that we have more
  reasons for coming together and healing than for staying alienated and stuck in pain. Drawing on our spiritual resources, we touch a far deeper basis for resolving
  disharmonies among us, and this awareness moves us
  toward inner peace.

Using the four to develop our potentials

Relative to the job of peacemaking Circles, the power of the Medicine Wheel's teaching lies in its capacity to remind us not only of
who we are but also of who we can become. Whether or not we

develop all four dimensions of our nature equally, we nonetheless possess them as potentials we can draw upon. By engaging all four in some measure, Circles help us tap our potentials to change.

The case of a somewhat sulky young man, Dave, illustrates how seeking balance among these four dimensions can catalyze positive shifts. The Circle was having trouble connecting with Dave. His head was down, and he mumbled. He wasn't engaging and seemed intent on keeping it that way. In a passing comment, though, Dave mentioned his running ability. A younger Circle member spontaneously asked if he'd like to race. Immediately, the teenager perked up and started tying his shoes. Laughing and teasing, the whole Circle went outside, and people set up start and finish lines on the street. The group was able to connect on a physical level when the mental and emotional levels were falling flat. Naturally, the physical interaction alone wasn't sufficient, but it provided a base from which the Circle could build the emotional, mental, and spiritual connections that Dave needed to turn his life around.

Because the experience of being in Circle engages the whole person, not only victims and offenders but everyone involved can gain a greater sense of balanced selfhood. Barry recounts how this has been true for him:

> In Circles, I found a balance. There was room for me both as a judge and as a person. My legal training and court-developed skills for analysis were needed and respected, yet equally important were the full range of my emotions. Since my first Circle, my tears have flowed freely over the pain, struggles, and courage expressed. So often in Circles, a spiritual feeling—a spiritual connection to others or to life—arises within me, often without my realizing it until after it happens. In Circles, I have experienced other professionals finding and expressing all dimensions of their being as well.

The authors of *The Sacred Tree: Reflections on Native American Spirituality,* Judie Bopp, Michael Bopp, Lee Brown, and Phil Lane Jr., explain the role of the Medicine Wheel in helping us develop our potentials—sides of ourselves that are hidden and perhaps unknown to us:

> When the medicine wheel is used as a mirror by sincere human beings, it shows that within them are hidden many wonderful gifts that have not yet been developed. For the medicine wheel can show us not only as we are now, but also as we could be if we were to develop the potential gifts the Creator has deposited within us.
>
> Many of these hidden potentialities might never be developed if we did not somehow discover and nurture them, for as the great spiritual teachers have taught, all the gifts a person potentially possesses are like the fruits hidden within the tree. . . .
>
> The medicine wheel can be used as a model of what human beings could become if they decided and acted to develop their full potential.[19]

EXPLORING INSTEAD OF CONQUERING DIFFERENCES

As we feel more grounded in our wholeness and connected to our potentials, we also feel more equipped to deal with complex situations. The shift to a holistic view of both ourselves and crime gives us the inner security to approach conflicts not as conquerors but as explorers. We ask such questions as: What potentials may lie hidden in this conflict? What possibilities might emerge if we could bring more of our wholeness to how we work this out?

The conventional approach to conflict is to reduce it to simple, manageable terms that fit our categories and then to fight the conflict with the aim to subdue it. We want to conquer the situation, so we can go back to life as it was before or so that we can feel vindicated in our view. If we're one of the key players, a conquering stance makes us want to leave the conflict as the winner, not the loser. If there are differences, we want to prove that we're right and the others—cast in the role of "opponents" or even "enemies"—are wrong.

A Circle philosophy invites a different approach. We listen to conflicts to discover the potentials for positive change that they may hold for us. Conflicts are openings, doorways to new ways of being together. Because they occur within the whole, they bear a meaning that in some way relates to the whole. Perhaps the way things were wasn't entirely working; conflicts invite us to explore how to change them. Perhaps we've accepted norms that conflicts call us to reevaluate.

Finding unexpected problems

If we enter Circles with an open, exploratory mind-set, we're more likely to uncover the deeper problems and to find deeper solutions. In every sentencing Circle we've experienced, no one coming into the Circle could have anticipated what later came out of it. Though the dialogue may start around the surface issues of a crime, as the buried stories of individuals and families come to light, the concerns soon expand beyond the legally defined issues.

In the case of Caroline, a young girl on the street charged with selling drugs, for instance, the Circle discovered that her mother was selling drugs too and that both were being forced to sell them by the mother's husband. Her mother was in denial. Caroline loved her mother and knew that telling the police about the situation would destroy a relationship that was important to her mother. The Circle arranged for Caroline to live with the family of her best friend in a funded placement program. They held a private Circle with the

mother and Caroline, which gave the mother the support and courage to leave the relationship. They found a temporary home for the
mother as well. Through the support of the Circle, both Caroline
and her mother entered drug treatment programs. In other words,
Caroline's "sentence" addressed her needs, not just her crime. It was
designed to reconnect a young woman with her potentials and to
the constructive energies of her life. The peacemaking agreement
that constituted her sentencing stretched beyond her and her crime
to include her mother, her friend, and, through community service
work, her community.

Working out unexpected solutions— solutions to life beyond the crime

Circles invite participants to sit with issues in all their facets and
then to explore together where a full awareness of the problem
may lead—and no one knows where that may be. Again, solutions
are often entirely different from what anyone originally thought.

Another case illustrates how deeply a Circle's journey must
sometimes go into the questions of life. George, seventeen, was ar-
rested for possessing a large quantity of illegal mushrooms. He was
caught when he drove his car off the road. He had been high for
days. In a Circle dealing with his charges, George wasn't responsive
to community members' concerns about his distributing drugs to
other teenagers—namely, their children. Nor was he responsive to
community concerns about his dangerous driving. Although not
the subject of the charge, his dangerous driving was well known in
the community. George sat in sullen silence and contributed very
little. Circle members grew frustrated and impatient. Their anger
finally prompted George to say, "I don't care about death. Dying
doesn't bother me. I just care about having as much fun as I can."

The dialogue abruptly changed. Participants spoke to his indifference not just to them but to life itself. Many remembered

their teenage angst and were now hearing similar attitudes from their own children. The new focus produced a very different outcome. The ultimate consensus targeted neither his dangerous driving nor his mushroom use but rather the underlying causes; namely, his indifference to life and hence his pursuit of reckless, even dangerous thrills. The sentence of the Circle, inspired in large part by George himself, was to complete a twelve-week hospice training. He did that and much more. After completing the training, for example, George volunteered to attend a ten-day intensive meditation retreat.

As in George's case, when a Circle creates a place safe enough for people to search their lives and share their stories, the dialogue can explore how to cure deep wounds. Though the crime isn't forgotten, the Circle treats it as a symptom of deeper causes and hence as a catalyst for deep change. While George's "sentence" was unorthodox in criminal justice terms, it was completely in accord with community interests, and in the long run, it advanced the overriding objectives of the criminal justice process far more than traditional sentences could have done.

What's most unexpected: our capacities to resolve conflicts peacefully

These remarkable resolutions come from the unexpected shifts that happen in Circles. Yet such shifts are precisely what Circles are designed to invite. They move everyone to a different place inwardly—one that's more open and authentic. As a result, we're able to connect more profoundly than we normally do. People who come in polarized and angry over an injustice, for example, find themselves working through problems in ways they couldn't anticipate. In Circles, coming up with answers is often the lesser part of resolving conflicts; the greater part is learning how to explore differences peacefully—with respect, honesty, humility, and all the other values. To an adversarial way of thinking, these outcomes aren't just unexpected, they're unimaginable.

By introducing new possibilities for working things out, Circles foster genuine and often intense cooperative learning. As we listen to each other, we get to know who others are beyond their roles and stereotypes, and we begin to see more sides of an issue. This expanded awareness enables us to "show up" differently in our interactions. We become less reactive to appearances and more responsive to needs and inner experiences. Others feel the shift in us to a deeper sensitivity and openness, and they in turn respond differently too.

In short, Circles aren't about performance or saying the right thing or making a good show. They're not about coming up with "*the* answer" and certainly not about getting others to think as we do. They're not even about forcing anyone to change. These are all techniques of conquering a situation—taking charge and fixing it. Instead, Circles are about going to the roots of our being, searching our hearts, souls, and truths, and rediscovering the values that help us express how we most want to be.

Of course, doing this is easier to describe than to do. Circles invite us deeper into our own hearts and lives, but it often takes time for us to respond to this call. Instead of coming to Circles with high-flown expectations, therefore, we try to maintain a balanced sense of what Circles can do, neither hoping too much nor putting a ceiling on what's possible. Circles are a profoundly human process, which means they have both potentials and limits.

Mindful of both, we can enter a Circle with openness to the process, trusting it and letting it take us to new places of awareness, discovery, learning, transformation, and healing. Circles are truly explorations into the unknown of who we can be and of what can happen when we connect from our core.

Chapter Three

The Outer Frame of Circles

> *This is terribly counter cultural, because we want quick*
> *fixes. We are all starving for community. Circle is a*
> *wonderful place to go and say something and know*
> *you'll be heard. It gives us a way to work things out*
> *other than just dividing people into "us" and "them."*
>
> —MINISTER AND CIRCLE PARTICIPANT

ALL THE ELEMENTS THAT MAKE UP the inner frame of Circles—
choosing peacemaking values, adhering to guiding principles, balancing the four fundamental aspects of our being, and exploring
instead of conquering our conflicts—may make Circles seem a
bit daunting. They're not. Most people find them a natural environment, perhaps because of their ancient origins. Even so, we
often need outer supports in practicing our inner ideals. It's easy
to get lost—to stray from how we most want to be—especially
when we're faced with conflicts. Circles provide a gentle, nonhier-
archical, respectful, yet highly effective support through five key
elements, which together establish the more visible, outer frame
for Circle dialogue:

Circle keeping. Keepers don't control the Circle but help participants uphold its integrity. They function supportively as servants
and midwives to whatever the Circle needs to do.

The talking piece. The talking piece creates a space for deep listening, so that each person's voice can be heard.

Guidelines. The guidelines form a collectively constructed, com-
monly understood ground of conduct.

Ceremonies. The ceremonies use inclusive, nondenominational, non-threatening rituals to help move people into the Circle space and then out of it again. Ceremonies promote a sense of community—of pulling together around shared visions, aims, and endeavors—within the Circle.

Consensus decision-making. Making decisions by consensus both honors the principles and values of Circles and helps participants stay grounded in them.

A tree offers a useful image of how the inner and outer frames work together. Circles grow from the root of shared values, guiding principles, and the teachings of the Medicine Wheel. From these roots, the keepers, the talking piece, the guidelines, the ceremonies, and consensus decision-making provide the strength—the sturdy, supportive trunk and branches—of the Circle gathering. The leaves and fruit that grow from them represent the effects we seek: the connections we make, the community building that goes on, and the healing that occurs as a natural outcome.

CIRCLE KEEPING: FACILITATING A SAFE SPACE FOR DIALOGUE

Keepers are the caretakers and servants of the Circle. Their presence is humble, supportive, and as unassuming as oil in an engine. They don't run the Circle but help participants do so. Their only power is what the Circle provides. Instead of taking charge or trying to influence how things go, keepers facilitate a balanced dialogue. "I learned very quickly," a participant in a youth Circle said, "that keepers show leadership first by living the values of a Circle and then by helping create the space for others to take leadership."

Keepers help hold a space that's clear, open, respectful, and free. They do so principally by trusting the Circle process to draw out

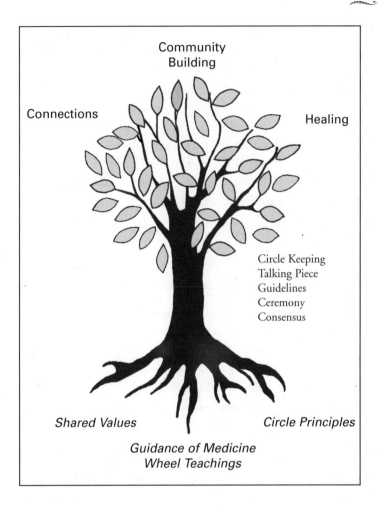

Community
Building

Connections

Healing

Circle Keeping
Talking Piece
Guidelines
Ceremony
Consensus

Shared Values   *Circle Principles*

Guidance of Medicine
Wheel Teachings

the wisdom of participants. If the ceremonies, guidelines, talking piece, and underlying Circle values are understood and accepted, keepers create an environment that encourages participants to share what's within them in ways they may not otherwise do.

Being a keeper isn't, therefore, about being charismatic or taking charge. It's not even about being a mediator or group facilitator, though these skills come in handy. It's about radically respecting the power of human beings and of Circles to deal with whatever is before them. One keeper said, "Keepers are really servants of the Circle. They do not run the Circle; they serve the Circle. It's not a position of power; it is a responsibility to others."

After all, why would we bother holding a Circle if keepers could wave their wands and fix things? And what would "fixing things" mean? How would relationships get built and trust in them grow? How would we feel empowered to take charge of our lives and communities, if keepers could step in and make problems go away? Circles are not about one person working miracles but about a community working them. Circles aim to build relationships, and this can be done only by participants actually doing it—learning from each other, practicing respect and honesty, expressing tough emotions, and through it all, gaining trust not only in themselves and others but also in their joint ability to work things out in a good way.

Since everyone in the Circle shares the charge to hold a safe, respecting space, everyone serves, in a sense, as co-keepers. "Everyone in the Circle is a keeper," one keeper observed, "and keepers need to ensure that everyone understands that. Just as the Circle belongs to everyone, everyone has a responsibility to help keep the Circle a safe place." The more keepers assume a high profile in running the Circle, the less participants feel like co-keepers. But the more keepers step back and let the Circle work through problems in its own way, the more participants share ownership for what goes on, take initiative in keeping the experience constructive, and commit themselves to making outcomes work. Carolyn Boyes-Watson, director of the Center for Restorative Justice at Suffolk University in Boston, Massachusetts, and author of *Holding the Space: The Journey of Circles at Roca*, observes, "Sitting in Circle often demonstrates the wisdom that 'everyone brings gifts' and that the power and wisdom come from the group rather than the 'leader.'"[20]

For Kay, this feature of Circles and Circle keeping enabled her to engage in the practice in a way she had not felt comfortable doing with other forms of mediation or group facilitation:

> One of the things I have loved about Circle keeping is that I am not responsible for the outcome—that I don't have to make the Circle go to a certain place. As a facilitator in small groups, I often felt inadequate or unsuccessful, because the group didn't generate the expected product. But in Circles as a keeper, I'm not supposed to determine the outcome or move a group in a particular direction. It has been an enormous relief to me.

In this spirit, the best keepers perform their work almost invisibly. They create spaces for others to take power by including them in the various tasks of the Circle. For example, they arrange for participants to welcome others, prepare refreshments, explain guidelines, conduct an introductory round, and plan the opening and closing ceremonies. Coordinating all this means that the keepers' work is largely done outside the Circle, both before and after.

What qualities characterize a good keeper? Fairness, integrity, skills in facilitating difficult conversations, knowledge of the community, empathy, humility, and patience: all of these qualities serve. Above all, keepers need to understand the values, principles, and practices of peacemaking Circles. As one keeper stated, "I don't do Circles; I aspire to live my life in Circle."

Keepers serve the Circle process in many ways, including:

1. *Preparing for the Circle*

In using Circles for crime, most communities choose two keepers several weeks before a Circle is scheduled. Preparation is essential for a constructive Circle gathering—a subject we will return to in greater depth in chapter 5—and it's the keepers' job to make sure all the bases are well covered in advance.

To start, keepers prepare themselves. They engage in ongoing inner work, which means regularly checking their thoughts and behavior against their core values and Circle principles. In Circles, whatever is within tends to come out, if not in words then nonverbally. Since keepers help set the tone, their inner attitude should be as aligned with the inner frame of Circles as possible. Just before a Circle gathering, keepers take time to center themselves and cultivate inner peace. Some take a walk in nature, others do meditation, breathing exercises, stretching, prayer, or listening to relaxing music. Inner quieting helps them become clearer vessels for the flow of a Circle.

In the weeks before the gathering, the keepers work together to prepare others for the Circle. They

- help identify who needs to be there;
- explain to participants how Circles work;
- find out what the issues, concerns, and needs are;
- discuss guidelines and ask participants what guidelines will make the Circle safe for them;
- explain their role as keepers;
- begin building relationships with participants;
- determine if preliminary Circles of healing or support are needed; and
- help decide when it feels right for offenders or victims to go ahead with a full Circle.

2. Providing equal access to information

For people to be equally empowered to participate, they need equal access to information *before* the Circle gathering. Keepers either provide this information or prompt others to share it. For instance, in sentencing Circles, keepers put everyone on an equal footing by giving community participants all the information that justice professionals have. This includes information such as presentence reports, criminal records, letters of support, and victim-impact statements.

3. Setting the tone

During the preparation stage, keepers set the tone for the Circle by answering questions, explaining all aspects of the process, and arranging help for anyone who needs it in preparing for the gathering. From the moment people enter the place for a Circle, keepers attend to creating a safe and welcoming atmosphere. They make sure that everyone is greeted warmly. By inviting others to perform different functions in advance, they encourage a sense of shared responsibility. In rounds of the talking piece that involve expressing deeper feelings, keepers may go first to show that it's safe to be vulnerable. In rounds that involve expressing views or opinions, they may speak last to lend balance at the end by expressing respect for all sides. In their summaries after each round or phase, keepers set a constructive tone by affirming everyone's courage to be honest and by valuing everyone's contribution, whether a consensus was achieved or not. Throughout, keepers strive to convey an atmosphere that's open, calm, unhurried, reflective, respectful of differing views, and appreciative of each person's efforts.

4. Facilitating Circle dialogue

If keepers have done a thorough job of preparation, they won't have much actual facilitating to do in the Circle. The talking piece and the guidelines channel the energies in good ways. Even in difficult times, as long as the guidelines are being followed, the more experienced keepers let the Circle deal with the issues in its own way. Those who become too proactive—too eager to "make things work out"—weaken the budding sense of collective accountability for the dialogue. Rose Wilson, a Yukon keeper, observed, "The more I served as a keeper, the more I learned to trust the Circle." Trusting the Circle to do the work empowers participants to accept responsibility for the peacemaking process, to solve problems together, and to do it without relying on experts. Empowering people and communities is the larger "solution" that Circles aim to achieve.

Naturally, keepers sometimes need to facilitate dialogue, yet there are many nonintrusive ways of doing it. They can hold the talking piece to open the Circle for free discussion or brainstorming. Or they can pass the talking piece to someone to start a new round with a specific question for participants to address. By posing a question that inspires storytelling and then modeling a response, keepers can facilitate a level of sharing that creates bonds of empathy and understanding. They can promote dialogue through their summaries at the end of rounds, when they express appreciation for how hard everyone has worked. Finally, keepers can call for breaks to allow for private discussions and to give everyone an emotional rest. During breaks, keepers can find out if anyone needs help or support.

5. *Balancing interests and perspectives*

During preparation, keepers try to ensure that all the interests involved in the situation will be represented. Then, in the thick of Circle work, keepers use their knowledge of the community to sense whether or not the dialogue is in fact balanced: Are all interests being adequately expressed? Are all voices being heard? Are some concerns missing from an emerging consensus? If so, keepers use breaks to encourage participants to express difficult feelings, to remind them that other lives are affected, and to suggest proposals that more fully integrate all interests.

6. Protecting the integrity of the process

For Circles to get at the roots of conflict and crime, we need to say the difficult things and to voice our intense feelings. Circles will often have explosive or emotionally draining moments, since they're designed to hold our most difficult conversations. Before, during, and after these intense moments, keepers can take various measures to maintain the Circle's integrity.

For example, focusing on the values and reaching agreement on the guidelines at the outset prevents most problems, which arise more from old habits than from intentional disrespect. Modeling appropriate conduct, gentle reminders, humor, and some forms of body language are other ways to respond to breaches of Circle guidelines. Keepers can also speak to people privately during breaks—to acknowledge the intense emotions and difficult dialogue as well as to ask for help in working things through in a good way.

Outright disruptive conduct, though, can't be ignored, and if no one else steps forward to remind the group of the guidelines, keepers should do so. As participants accept their role as co-keepers, they help do this. Most of all, keepers develop both a tolerance for emotionally difficult moments and a trust that the Circle can work through them. From such moments, Circles can work miracles.

7. Regulating the pace of the Circle

Circle dialogues can be intense and emotionally draining, and it can take time to do a round. Keepers need to sense when the pace needs to shift.

If, for example, a participant holding the talking piece speaks at great length, others can grow uneasy. Naturally, if a long speech

involves a deep and personal outpouring of the heart, it's best not
to interrupt. But other times a keeper may feel a need to intervene. Circle participants can become absorbed in speaking and
may appreciate reminders of the guideline about pacing their
time talking. Sometimes Circles use two talking pieces, one for
the Circle and one for the keeper. By raising his or her talking
piece, the keeper signals that the Circle's talking piece needs to
move on. Some Circles even have special guidelines that require
keepers to curtail long-winded speakers. The best way to avoid
unduly long speeches, though, is to explain the need for respectful pacing up front.

If keepers choose to deal with a lengthy speech by calling for
a break, they can ask the speaker if he or she wishes to finish now
or to do so after the break. During the break, the keeper can remind the speaker of the time needed for others to participate.
Agreeing initially to break every sixty to ninety minutes can help
solve such problems. On returning, keepers can start again on a
positive note, reminding the Circle of any time constraints and of
everyone's need to talk. Participants can then pace themselves so
that everyone has a chance to speak before the Circle closes.

8. *Welcoming new people*

Though Circles can be a one-time response to an event, most
Circle programs that deal with crime meet regularly. As we will
explain later on, a core group takes responsibility for keeping the
process going. In the course of development, new people may attend, coming either to support key players or to see if they want
to become regular community volunteers. Whenever new people
show up, keepers make sure that they understand how a Circle
works and the framework in which they'll be participating. Then
keepers either introduce them or start a round of introductions.
When people arrive late, one of the keepers can leave the Circle

to welcome them and brief them about what has taken place. Everyone must feel welcomed, and all the participants can help create this welcoming atmosphere, especially by sharing the responsibility of greeting newcomers.

9. Maintaining focus

In preparation Circles, in meetings with key participants beforehand, as well as in full Circle gatherings, keepers help a Circle stay focused on the issues. They do this by posing questions or themes for a round and by providing summaries at the beginning, throughout, and at the end of Circles.

What's an appropriate focus for Circles that deal with crime? Peacemaking Circles are interested not just in formulating a sentence but in supporting victims and offenders and in finding out what caused a crime; hence, the issues are defined not by the laws involved but by the people involved. Circles may originally focus on the harm done but then shift to addressing the crime's underlying causes, as in George's case with his issues around life and death. Circles may also explore ways to help those harmed reconnect with friends and community. Looking to the future, Circles may focus on how to make changes in personal lives as well as in the community that will prevent further harms.

In other words, to take a holistic approach, Circles need to explore all aspects of a situation, some of which may at first seem irrelevant. Respecting this need, keepers are careful not to maintain a focus too rigidly. Crime typically raises complex personal, family, economic, and social problems, and the issues that at first seem most critical can shift radically.

In a Circle dealing with a single mother's drunk-driving charge, for example, the Circle soon discovered that Joan was caught in a desperate personal struggle that led to suicidal tendencies and child neglect. Participants then discovered that Joan's extended family and community had failed to recognize the needs of this mother lost in her battle to survive. While maintaining a focus is important, keepers are also mindful of life's complexities and that crime never occurs in a vacuum. The unique effectiveness of Circles lies precisely in their capacity to address a conflict in all its dimensions.

10. Participating as themselves

Though keepers don't use their position to impose their views, they are nonetheless contributing members of the Circle. Keepers are participants too, just as participants are co-keepers. In rounds of the talking piece, keepers speak from their own voice as a person. They don't try to maintain a detached, observer role, which would be contrary to the values of inclusivity, equality, and sharing. They engage in the Circle process just like everyone else, which includes stating perceptions, expressing emotions, and sharing personal stories.

In courts and in professional conflict-resolution practices, judges, arbitrators, facilitators, and mediators are trained not to become personally involved. They're expected to hold themselves apart as objective, neutral, unbiased observer-experts. Circles treat issues around neutrality and bias differently. Instead of asking keepers to disconnect equally from all parties, Circles call upon keepers to make an equal commitment to each participant in the quest to respect all interests. Equal commitment serves a process devoted to building relationships better than a strategy of detached neutrality, which would be inconsistent with the Circle view that all things are connected and cannot be separated. One First Nation keeper expressed how she deals with this issue:

> This Circle is about people I know and care about, people I work with. It is about my community. Of course it af-

fects me. Of course I've got feelings about this. It would
not be a true thing if I pretended not to have these feelings. The only thing is, as a keeper, maybe I've got to be
more careful how and when I express myself. I have to
be sure I offer everyone an opportunity to be respected,
and that what I share in the Circle is done in a good and
respectful way. But it needs to be shared. In the Circle, we
all must be present to what takes place. I'm not just there
as a keeper. I'm there as myself as well, and often opening
up my feelings is more important than being a keeper. If
the Circle is really as it should be, we are all keepers.

In short, when participants are aligned with the values, principles,
philosophy, and practices of Circles, most Circles evolve naturally,
and keepers need to do very little to generate a balanced, inclusive,
and productive dialogue. Once again, the less keepers do to "run
the Circle," the more participants share responsibility for how it
goes, the more everyone experiences the Circle as a genuine community endeavor, and the more participants commit themselves
to the outcomes.

THE TALKING PIECE: ENSURING EQUAL CONTRIBUTION AND A REFLECTIVE PACE

While the basic concept of the talking piece is simple—speak only
when the talking piece is passed to you—its impact on Circle dialogue is multifaceted and profound. The talking piece generates
and then sustains an inclusive dialogue. To those who are quiet,
shy, or struggling to find their voice in a group space, the talking
piece offers an opportunity to share what's on their minds and
hearts. Conversely, to those accustomed to asserting their views,
the talking piece offers an opportunity to listen and ponder. The

talking piece opens doors of communication not only outwardly among those in the Circle but also inwardly for each participant by lending a focus for inner reflection. The talking piece fosters the deep listening that's a hallmark of Circles. As the talking piece moves around the Circle, people listen in a heartfelt way that connects and heals.

Not everyone finds such deep and extended listening easy to do. Blaise Pascal, the seventeenth-century French philosopher, quipped, "I have discovered that all human evil comes from this, man's being unable to sit still in a room." And he's right: it can be difficult. Initially, some fidget or become anxious as they wait for what can seem like "forever to get [their] hands on the talking stick." Accustomed to challenging anyone's air space with comments that can't wait, people often don't realize how their interruptions shut others down.

When peacemaking Circles are used for crime, lawyers and judges often have trouble containing their need to make a point. Respecting their experience in the court culture and the professional pressures that led them to develop these patterns, keepers can remind them of Circle guidelines and ask them to be patient.

With time, though, even those most keen to get their hands on the talking stick discover the transformative power of listening. One prosecutor observed that "the feather forced me to listen, and really listening in the Circle changed me—changed my perspective. Others said what I needed to say better than I could. And I really did not feel the responsibility was just mine. It was somehow shared."

Hearing each other's stories moves us both closer together and closer to ourselves. A community member observed, "I got a deeper sense of myself listening to the stories of [others] in the Circle." For many, the quiet, respectful listening brings deep healing. When we see our own stories reflected in those of others, we feel connected, and pain we've carried for years begins to heal. Another community

member said, "Knowing that others had walked and were walking
the same path helped me immensely, not just to understand [her]
but to know that others were carrying the same stuff. It was like a
healing." Sharing personal stories has the power to be life-giving
as well as life-changing. When we recognize our own lives, pain,
hopes, and struggles in the stories of others, we understand each
other and connect—often for the first time.

Being heard in a quiet, respectful way can be equally powerful.
In her article "Good Listening," adapted from her recent book
*Turning to One Another: Simple Conversations to Restore Hope to
the Future,* organizational consultant Margaret J. Wheatley writes:

> One of the easiest human acts is also the most healing.
> Listening to someone. Simply listening. Not advising or
> coaching, but silently and fully listening. . . .
>
> Why is being heard so healing? I don't know the full
> answer to that question, but I do know it has something
> to do with the fact that listening creates relationship. . . .
> In the web of life, nothing living lives alone.
>
> Our natural state is to be together. Though we keep
> moving away from each other, we haven't lost the need to
> be in relationship. Everybody has a story, and everybody
> wants to tell their story in order to connect. If no one lis-
> tens, we tell it to ourselves and then we go mad. . . .
>
> Listening moves us closer; it helps us become more
> whole, more healthy, more holy. Not listening creates
> fragmentation, and fragmentation always causes more suf-
> fering. . . . It is impossible to create a healthy culture if we
> refuse to meet, and if we refuse to listen. But if we meet,
> and when we listen, we reweave the world into wholeness.[21]

The talking piece helps us listen. Because of the order, rhythm,
and structure that the talking piece establishes, the attention we

give each other in Circles is unique. Our listening is respectful, reflective, and fully present. We're not distracted by feeling a need to respond, since the whole Circle is there to deal with whatever issues arise. From this depth of presence with each other, the listening we do in Circles heals, connects, and "reweaves the world into wholeness."

Using the talking piece

The talking piece creates this positive listening atmosphere when participants follow the conventions of its use:

- *The talking piece moves one way.* The talking piece moves in one direction around the Circle. Many northern First Nation communities move it clockwise, following the path of the Sun. The talking piece doesn't jump around but goes consistently all the way around the Circle to ensure that everyone gets a chance to speak. It creates a pattern of listening before speaking and then listening again.

- *People speak only when holding the talking piece.* People are encouraged to speak only when holding the talking piece, except when the keeper indicates otherwise (see below). Following this guideline, participants learn the importance of waiting to speak, which creates better listening skills. The talking piece imposes no obligation to talk. It can be passed without speaking or held to give the Circle a moment of shared silence. Holding the talking piece can create a powerful moment.

    For example, when the talking piece came to her, Jessie, an Elder, simply held the feather for awhile. She then explained to Jack, the young offender next to her, that she was creating moments of silence for him to prepare to speak: "We want to hear from you. I am holding on to this feather to give you time to find your voice, so you can speak from your heart. We're all here to help you. You know I love you. I know you have a good heart. Let us hear from your good heart." Jack waited then nodded when he was ready. He spoke for the first time. Though he had never before spoken in court, he poured out his pain from his heart with an apology that was unmistakably genuine.

Once the talking piece has moved around the Circle and come back to the keeper, the keeper may

- summarize what has been shared in the Circle and raise further questions before passing the talking piece around again;
- hold it and call upon specific participants to clarify points or respond to particular issues;
- pass it to someone else to start another round of the Circle. Since the person sitting to the left of the keeper may feel on the spot by always having to go first, the keeper may carry the talking piece to someone else. The talking piece need not start with the same person, but it should always move in the same direction;
- hold it and open the Circle for anyone to speak;
- place it in the center of the Circle for anyone to pick up and use to speak or to open the Circle for discussion without using the talking piece at all. In open exchanges, participants are still called to honor the Circle process by speaking truthfully, with respect, and without dominating the time. If a few people start to dominate or the energy of the exchanges becomes negative, reintroducing the talking piece restores balance.

Choosing a talking piece

The object that a community uses for a talking piece depends on the community's customs and traditions, on the nature of the issues, and on what will serve the Circle. A talking piece that's respected can help turn contentious debates into inclusive dialogues. It can inspire a spiritual connection within the Circle. And it can remind participants of Circle principles and values while they're speaking.

Because the talking piece can be a powerful symbol, communities invest time in choosing them. Choosing a talking piece that has a significance for the group generates a sense of respect for the process it creates. The object should remind participants to speak openly and honestly from the heart and to listen with the same openhearted attitude. The talking piece should be respected both inside and outside the Circle, and to support this regard, it should be kept in a special place when not in use.

Whatever the form, the talking piece should support the sense that the Circle is a sacred space. When an object is well-chosen for a group, the talking piece "pulls the goodness out of people," as Mark says. It calls us to deal with issues from the best in ourselves. As we do, we're more open to considering new ideas. Kay experienced a Circle in which the symbolic significance of the talking piece played a pivotal role:

> In a large, impersonal room in sweltering heat, I kept
> a Circle for eight staff members from a small charter
> school. I explained the Circle process and the use of a
> talking piece. The group had asked me to keep a Circle
> for them to deal with a painful internal conflict centered
> around one of the teachers. Someone brought a soft foam
> apple, symbolizing the role of the teacher, to be used as
> the talking piece. The group moved through introduc-

tions and tentative hints at the issues among the staff, but it was clear that the speaking was very guarded. No one addressed the principal problem.

After lunch, I introduced a new talking piece, a four-inch-long slender snail shell. I commented on the beauty of the snail shell even though it was broken, suggesting that the brokenness of the outer shell enabled us to see the lovely, delicate inner spiral of the shell. When the shell reached the woman at the center of the problems, she held the shell, and with tears in her eyes, spoke: "This talking piece is very powerful. I came today just to get through, to get it over with, to say as little as possible. I didn't plan to talk about how I felt. But this talking piece won't let me do that." She spoke from her heart in a way that opened up the dialogue and brought the problem fully into the Circle.

Choosing a talking piece within a community can provide another opportunity to discover common ground and to forge new connections. If a community doesn't have a talking piece, keepers may need to propose one. Circles choose a talking piece by consensus, so that everyone feels respect for it and knows what it signifies. When, for example, First Nation communities use a stone for a talking piece, they regard it not only as a stone but as something that has absorbed the wisdom and spirit of their ancestors.

Talking pieces may be feathers, stones, sticks, flowers, or anything that appropriately conveys a particular meaning to the Circle. One community uses a helix made from recycled pop cans. At the end of each Circle, the keepers present it to someone as a gift from the Circle. Another community allows for both a common and an individual talking piece. The common one is passed around the Circle in the normal way. Participants are invited to bring their own talking pieces to hold when the common talking piece reaches them. Sharing the significance of these personal talking pieces builds connections among the group.

The benefits of using a talking piece

Though simple enough as a practice, using a talking piece has a powerful effect in changing how a group interacts. It promotes open and constructive dialogue in many ways.

Promotes dialogue. Most directly, using a talking piece balances participation, so a few don't dominate. Those who otherwise may not speak have a chance to contribute. Because all voices are heard, more perspectives are offered. The talking piece carries an implicit message that each person has something important to contribute, and this message in turn encourages people to share their feelings. On a practical level, using a talking piece keeps contributions brief. Mindful that others are waiting to speak, the one holding the talking piece tends to pace his or her comments accordingly, following the model or time frame given by the keepers.

Affirms equality. Using a talking piece makes a powerful statement for equality. It opens the same space for each participant, making no distinction of rank, education, or power, and no preference for style, eloquence, or content. It also encourages participants to share responsibility for what happens in the Circle. The talking piece spreads ownership for the success of the dialogue to each participant. Everyone has a chance to help the Circle move through whatever challenges arise.

Slows the pace. Passing a talking piece also slows down the discussion. Knowing that the talking piece will hold the space until the speaker is finished, participants don't feel a need to talk rapidly. The pace becomes more relaxed and thoughtful. Everyone knows they'll have an uninterrupted chance to speak, and that when they speak, they can speak deliberately, assured that no one will break in or cut them off.

Develops listening skills. Using a talking piece fosters good listening skills. Since most of the time in Circles is spent listening, everyone grows more accustomed to doing it. We discover that others share similar thoughts and feelings, and this discovery builds connections. Listening also gives us a better understanding of our differences, not only in outward ways but also in how we think and feel.

Granted, many of us have learned to listen with our mouths. We look for openings to grab air time and react in the moment. Newcomers to the Circle often become frustrated waiting for the talking piece. Eventually, though, we discover that waiting brings deeper listening and genuine reflection, which changes the way we respond. Waiting and listening can not only bring out unexpected thoughts and feelings, but can also move us to more personal levels of sharing. The following comment by a community member describes some common reactions:

> I had been thinking of what I would say while waiting for the feather, you know, shaping what I would say to make people impressed by what I said. Then, without ever realizing it, I got caught up in listening to what others were saying. Suddenly the feather was in my hand, and what came out was nothing like what I had rehearsed to say. What came out was much more personal, much more honest. I was really surprised by what did come out of me.

Cultivates peacemaking abilities. Especially in Circles dealing with crime, using a talking piece helps participants learn peacemaking. When emotions run hot for key players, those less directly involved have a chance to deal with the emotions constructively and to act as peacemakers. They can acknowledge the anger, respect the concerns raised, and explore positive ways of channeling charged emotions. Anger isn't ignored but heard and processed by the whole Circle, while the person at whom the anger is directed feels less driven to respond in a highly charged way. By acknowledging the anger, suggesting constructive ways of dealing with it, and offering support for both sides, participants build the skills and capacity to move beyond the resentments that angry outbursts provoke.

For example, Jane, a community member whose friend's cabin had been broken into and ransacked by Jake, a young offender, was understandably angry. She let her emotions fly. Her own cabin had been ransacked the same way a year earlier. As the feather was passed around the Circle, participants digested her anger. They acknowledged her pain, but they also gave Jake and his parents an opportunity to respond in a good way by attesting to the difficulties that both youths and their parents face. Participants talked about the need for parents as well as community members to spend more time with young people. Hearing Jane's anger, Jake's father was initially angry in return, but his attitude changed: "I was ready to jump down her throat for speaking about my son in such a way. But as I waited to speak, I listened to people reaching out to help my family, to help my son deal with this in a good way. I spoke in a way that surprised me, and I think I set a better example for my son to speak. I was so proud of the way he spoke [in accepting responsibility]. I don't think he would have done so if I'd have ranted back at her."

Fosters honesty. A talking piece also reminds people to speak honestly, humbly, and authentically. As a symbol of Circle principles and values, the talking piece represents a collective commitment to search for truth, even if it means expressing the pain that truth often reveals. Holding the talking piece becomes a sacred call to speak the truth as best we see it. It also calls us to engage from our higher selves. This doesn't mean that we gloss over issues or hide uncomfortable feelings but that we deal with tough emotions from our hearts and according to our best values. A talking piece that symbolizes for us spiritual connectedness and higher principles encourages us to do this.

Supports conditions for consensus. By bringing everyone into the process and appealing to the best in us, the talking piece lays the foundation for forming a consensus. Through each round of the talking piece, hostilities yield to understanding, and areas of common ground begin to emerge. We build on each other's input, slowly weaving the threads of our diverse contributions into a consensus.

For all these reasons, a talking piece is indispensable for generating a respectful, reflective dialogue in highly emotional situations. By shifting power and responsibility from a few key people to everyone in the Circle, the talking piece spreads leadership equally and draws everyone into the process. Using a talking piece can transform hostilities and resolve impasse in ways that reveal our sacredness—our capacities to be more than we appear, even to ourselves. A Lakota Circle keeper says, "In a Circle, when each person speaks with the talking piece, it's like a prayer."

Guidelines: Agreeing to Come Together "In a Good Way"

Circle guidelines are much more than directions for facilitating a meeting. They reflect the values and principles of the Circle process, both in their content (what they say) and in their relationship to participants (how they're used). In their content, the core guidelines translate Circle principles into practice. They describe how to be in Circle by putting our shared values into action. In their relationship to participants, the guidelines broadly frame the Circle process without being rigid or inflexible. Reflecting the open-ended, noncontrolling character of Circles, the guidelines align us with the spirit of Circles but allow participants to decide how to apply them.

During the opening phase of a Circle, keepers explain how guidelines and values are connected: guidelines help participants put their personal values into practice. In this context, guidelines are seen not as rigid rules imposed from without but as rooted in

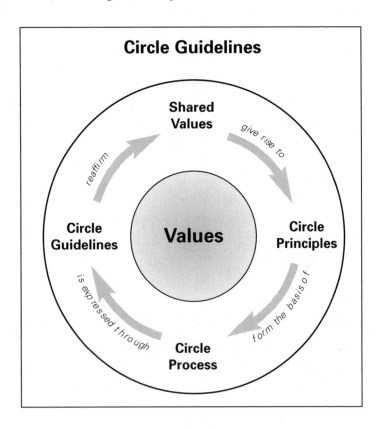

each person's own values. When Circles view the guidelines this way, participants more naturally hold the guidelines' form and spirit together and are less likely to experience them as school-room strictures.

Keepers explain the core guidelines to participants during the preparation stage, so everyone understands them before they walk in. When the Circle convenes, keepers begin by seeking consensus on the guidelines, asking for additional suggestions on creating a safe and respectful place for the conversation at hand. Right from the start, everyone is involved in the process, because they have a say in deciding what the process will be.

Beginning a Circle by "talking about how to talk" serves various functions beyond setting the parameters for conduct. If we "talk about how to talk" up front, everyone understands how we want to interact, and we agree to share responsibility for the process. We give opposing parties a chance to find common ground—to experience coming to an agreement before we get down to the more fractious issues. And we give participants their first experience of a Circle approach: a respect for all interests, a call for everyone to share responsibility for the process, and a commitment to making decisions through consensus. In other words, we not only build a desire for peacemaking but also demonstrate how it can work within the Circle space.

When, for example, the victim of a "break and enter" was able to actively participate in shaping the guidelines, she felt "as if [the Circle] did not just belong to the offender but to me—that was the turning point for my participation." "I didn't know the Circle would be so much different from court," one offender said. "I'd had several court experiences, you know. Each time I sat through with nothing to say, nothing to do about what happened, so I was surprised to find out before the Circle even started that I got a say about how it could be safe for me."

Along with additional guidelines participants may agree upon for a specific Circle, the following six guidelines are essential for Circle dialogues. Collectively, they translate the values and principles into concrete behavior that makes it easy for newcomers to adapt to the Circle atmosphere. These core guidelines are:

- respect the talking piece;
- speak from the heart;
- speak with respect;
- listen with respect;
- remain in the Circle; and
- honor confidentiality.

Respect the talking piece

By respecting the talking piece (i.e., not talking when someone else is holding it), we show respect for each others' views and perspectives. When everyone has an equal opportunity to speak, we acknowledge each other's need to express our thoughts and feelings without worrying about being interrupted. In a practical way, respect for the talking piece shows that we value inclusivity. It also inspires listening and reflection, giving us a chance to hear many voices and to find thoughts and words we didn't know we had.

Speak from the heart

In calling everyone to speak from the heart, the second guideline draws on many Circle values: honesty, trust, sharing, courage, and humility, perhaps also empathy, forgiveness, and love. Following this guideline helps us find ways to express pain and anger in a good way. Instead of accusing or blaming others, for example, we share our feelings and state plainly how words, actions, or events have affected us.

When offenders speak from their hearts in Circles, they're often much more honest than they'd ever be in courts. One offender described the difference: "Getting into the stand was like getting ready to play the game. It was your one chance not to tell your story but to make points with the judge. In the Circle, I knew lies and half-truths wouldn't cut it. That's because I felt people were listening, not to figure out what sentence I would get, but to hear who I was. I had to put me in there—not someone I wanted them to think I was, but who I really was. If I didn't, I knew it would be a game I'd play, and they'd all play."

In Circles, no one is asked to take an oath. Keepers explain that holding the talking piece is the same as giving an oath. The talking piece calls on us to speak the truth wholeheartedly, and holding the talking piece symbolizes our personal commitment to doing this.

Speak with respect

This guideline asks us to share our feelings in a respectful way, both in what we say and in how we say it. Brevity, for instance, sends its own message of respect—that other voices are worth hearing too.

In Circles, difficult things need to come out, but we can strive to say them in a respectful way. The desire to do this comes from our values. Our honesty doesn't stand alone. Humility, empathy, respect, and love make us want to consider how others might experience our words, while courage, trust, and often love make us want to speak our truth even if we know it'll be difficult for us to say and for others to hear.

In speaking with respect, we honor our differences. We can differ without being difficult, pursue our interests without diminishing the interests of others, and express our beliefs without showing disrespect for other ideas. Indeed, the strength of Circles lies in their capacity to consider more than one viewpoint. Speaking about our differences in a good way—with openness, honesty, consideration, and receptivity to perspectives other than our own—invites others to do the same.

Listen with respect

The guideline of listening with respect comes from our values too. Inclusivity makes us want to include more perspectives than our own. Humility does as well, because it reminds us that our views are limited and that we need the help of others to enlarge our understanding. Empathy—the desire to experience what others feel—inspires us to listen respectfully, which helps us forgive ourselves and others and hence to feel a greater sense of love.

Our whole body communicates these values by how we listen. Instead of interrupting, showing disinterest through body language, or whispering to others when someone is speaking, we demonstrate respectful listening skills by focusing our minds, bodies, and hearts on receiving what another is saying. Attending to how we listen conveys respect for others and the process, and it supports a collective intention to work together in a good way.

Remain in the Circle

Unless excused by a keeper, all participants are expected to remain in the Circle until it's over. Because Circles deal with emotions, personal stories, and volatile issues, participants need to stay together to work everything through, if not to full resolution, at least to some balanced stopping point. If a person explodes with rage and storms out, or if the one at whom anger is directed leaves, the conflict can't be processed safely and constructively in the Circle. One Circle participant commented, "When we come together, we are strong. Anyone leaving makes us much less than just one less."

Wanting to remain in the Circle, even when it feels hardest to do, comes from our values as well. For one thing, respect keeps us in the Circle. We know differences are real and that they help us learn and grow. Our honesty makes us want to know the truth beyond our own perspective. Growing trust in ourselves, in others, and in the Circle space gives us the courage to stay with the healing process.

Practical considerations help us remain in the Circle as well. People generally are more relaxed about "remaining in Circle" when they know the time limits, both how long the gathering will last and how often the group will take a break. During preparation and at the beginning of a Circle, keepers seek consensus around these issues. Honoring the agreed-upon time constraints reduces anxiety for participants, and they're able to "park" difficult emotions in a good way until the next Circle.

When people leave a Circle before its close, others often assume the worst. Someone might wonder, "Did she leave because of what I said?" when the woman really left because she had just remembered a dental appointment. To add flexibility to the guidelines, participants who must leave the Circle can be asked to step outside the Circle and quietly explain to the keeper what's going on. At an opportune time, keepers can then explain why someone left.

Timely breaks also help people remain in Circle by giving everyone an emotional breather. Key participants can carry intense or painful emotions out of the Circle without leaving it. One keeper commented, "I love breaks! It always feels as if people return ready for a lighter tone, a fresher start, and a new sense of resolve." However, using breaks to relieve intensities can be a tough call. Breaking too often takes the essential energy of difficult moments away from the Circle. It lessens the opportunities for growth, connection, and greater understanding that working through conflicts together can bring. Keepers must trust the Circle to do the hard work, and they gain this trust through experience: seeing one Circle after another pull positive energy and deep connections from tense or painful exchanges.

Honor confidentiality

What comes out in Circle stays in Circle. Respect, empathy, and love make us sensitive to the need for this guideline. We want confidentiality honored so we can share what's on our minds and hearts freely. Trust also makes us want this guideline, so we can be in a safe space: we know that what we say won't be repeated out of context or used against us.

This guideline has many exceptions, but it's the starting point for Circle dialogue. In the various Circles used to prepare people for a sentencing Circle, participants may agree to share any information generally or only with certain named others. Otherwise, everything expressed in these Circles stays in the Circle.

Confidentiality is different for sentencing Circles, because the law requires sentencing to be a public process. As a result, very little is confidential. Only personal stories and information collectively agreed to be kept confidential stay in the Circle. Stories can be shared only if the teller gives permission to do so.

A case involving sexual abuse illustrates how a Circle can agree to keep sensitive information confidential. A detailed psychological assessment of the offender and his family contained very personal information about his parents. The information could have been the subject of a successful court application to ban publication and/ or public exposure. The family wanted to honor the Circle and allow the participants to appreciate the full story. Someone from the media wanted to be part of the Circle. The Circle, including the media person, agreed to keep the psychological assessment confidential. The journalist wrote the full story of the Circle without breaking the confidentiality of the psychological report.

Circles need to talk about confidentiality up front. If someone in the Circle is legally required to report to the state any information he or she hears, participants need to know this from the outset. If necessary, the mandated reporter may leave the Circle when someone wants to divulge a crime or when a victim wants to share an experience but doesn't want to press charges. Whenever such information surfaces, the Circle assumes responsibility for arranging help for those who need it, whether victims or offenders, as well as for taking steps to rectify what has occurred and to prevent any further harm from happening.

In many communities, fewer than 40 percent of all crimes are reported to the police, and many reported crimes are not prosecuted. Circles are a way for communities to address the personal difficulties surrounding unresolved crimes. These crimes come to light in Circles in various ways. A husband dealing with a specific charge of spousal assault will acknowledge other incidents. Other men in the Circle will speak of their own violence within their families. Youths who come to support a friend on drug charges will admit their abuse too, while participants from the community will share their experiences of victimization.

All are seeking help, and their stories show community members that the problem facing them is much larger than the specific crime before the Circle. Though each case is different and may require a different response, these personal revelations are respected as they are intended; namely, as contributions to the Circle's healing work. The obvious exception to confidentiality usually involves personal or public safety, such as when a victim seeks additional formal sanctions or when a child or anyone else is in danger of further harm. No matter how the information is handled, though, such disclosures always trigger help by either the community, the state, or both.

Additional guidelines

Building on these core guidelines, communities may develop other guidelines that fit not only the community's circumstances but also the distinct needs and conditions of a case. During the course of a Circle, the call for another guideline may arise, and the participants may have another discussion about how to be together. As communities do this—add their own guidelines, practice them, refine them, and adapt them to specific cases—they develop a sense of ownership over the process. They make the Circle process their own. Each time a Circle is reconvened, the guidelines need to be reviewed. Talking about how to be together isn't a simple formality; it's a ceremony of mutual commitment to make and share a sacred space.

Additional Circle guidelines sometimes cover logistical matters, such as using special talking pieces, limiting Circle sessions to three hours, sharing a meal before or after a Circle, engaging two or more keepers, arranging special seating for key participants, and agreeing to meet again. Other guidelines concern participants' attitude and conduct, such as not having hidden agendas, not being long-winded, refraining from name-calling, keeping an open mind, and believing in new beginnings. Being flexible about the guidelines ensures that the Circle fits both the community and the specific conflict.

Support keepers

When keepers discuss the guidelines during preparation and at the start of Circles, they need to explain their own functions as keepers and to ask the Circle to accept the guidelines that define their role. Keepers need the Circle's support in exercising their responsibilities. These responsibilities involve deciding

- when and how to interrupt;
- when to open the Circle and when to bring it to a close;
- when to take a break;
- how to use the talking piece; and
- how to remind people to adhere to the agreed-upon guidelines.

When keepers forget to begin by clarifying their role, misunderstandings may develop that undermine the Circle process.

Honor the guidelines

The guidelines aren't rules to be rigidly enforced. How they are applied depends mostly on the insight, intuition, and experience of the keepers. Setting a good example, gentle reminders, and private discussions during breaks are usually enough to keep everyone mindful of them. These tactful means enable keepers to avoid an atmosphere of "enforcing the law."

Ideally, other participants join in "keeping the Circle" by finding gentle, respectful ways to move past breaches. When keepers are patient and tolerant of minor slips, participants tend to take a more active role in helping others work through their emotions constructively, revealing the self-teaching, self-regulating, self-guiding capacity of Circles. As Circles become common practice within a community, respecting the guidelines ceases to be an issue.

Be flexible

Far from being rigid rules, Circle guidelines represent a dynamic consensus that responds to the changing circumstances of how participants want to be together. When participants choose to honor the guidelines, they take responsibility for their conduct, agreeing to be held accountable to their values and to their commitment to others. For many young people, developing and then following guidelines that honor everyone's need to participate is a new experience. Elizabeth Ba, a Cambodian and the director of the Lynn Leadership Program at Roca, comments:

> In school, people are never flexible, and the young people
> are never given the space to decide for themselves what
> the rules are or the idea that they can change those rules.
> Wow! To say, "I don't agree to this . . ." and to know that
> they would change for me! Or that I can challenge that
> [rule]. I think that the opportunity for us to be flexible
> with the guidelines is crucial, because if [the guidelines
> we're using] don't work, what other choices do we have?
> [Young people] don't experience this in the schools or
> their homes or anywhere in their lives.[22]

In her report on the use of Circles at Roca, Carolyn Boyes-Watson concludes:

> It is a profound lesson when young people and adults
> come to the realization that if living in accordance with
> the values is something they wish for, it is also something
> they must be responsible for.[23]

The guidelines honor the worth of each participant, protecting space for everyone's contribution. Circles need all the talents that people bring. A participant's special gift may be to tell stories, to be empathetic, to exercise analytic skills, to have the courage to speak candidly, to know intuitively what will move people closer to their best selves, or to sense how to offer love and support. Other gifts to the Circle may be expressed outside the gathering, such as having the commitment to get things done, knowing when to visit someone in need, learning how to organize and raise funds, preparing shared meals, or having the persistence to track down a resource. By drawing everyone into the process, the guidelines help every talent find its best expression within the larger Circle process.

CEREMONIES: MOVING US TO DEEPER PLACES

Ceremonies provide the fourth basic element of Circles to further frame the process. Our lives include all sorts of rituals—meaningful patterns of behavior that move us to an inward place which reflects how we want to be together. A hug is a ritual that affirms caring and closeness in a relationship. It's a common opening and closing ceremony that friends use to create a warm space of being together. Spending time with family or animal companions when we first come home helps us shift from the outside world of work, traffic, and schedules to the inside world of relaxation, nurturing, and intimacy.

Yet rituals and ceremonies get a bad name in Western culture, for various reasons. For one thing, we may not connect with the ritual's meaning, and so it feels empty. Or the ritual might convey a meaning we no longer relate to or don't like, and that's just as unhelpful. Since childhood, we may have felt pressured to follow rituals that seemed alien or contrived, in which case the message wasn't of a spiritual, soulful, or connecting nature but of a social expectation to conform—to connect with others at the price of disconnecting from ourselves. That's not good either.

To work well, rituals need to be voluntary, as with all aspects of Circle participation, and participants need to understand how they relate to shared principles and values. Considering the cross-cultural composition of many Circles, the rituals used in Circles often come from different cultures. This multicultural approach to ceremonies honors diverse traditions, as long as everyone understands the meaning behind a ritual, is comfortable with it, and feels totally free not to participate if they so choose.

In Circles, rituals and ceremonies serve many functions. They can be fun and relaxing. They can serve as ice-breakers and invite a deeper level of sharing. They can be deeply moving, or they can help us lighten up. Basically, like hugs between friends on meeting, Circle ceremonies move us to ways of being together that are different from what we were doing or feeling before.

Opening ceremonies

Opening ceremonies help us make the transition from the hurly-burly world of working, dealing with the kids, stewing about things, or feeling separate and on our own to the reflective Circle space. They help us shift inwardly from head to heart. Through an opening ritual, we begin to connect with others and to cultivate a sense of community within the Circle. We also begin to connect with ourselves. We feel more centered and open to inner peace.

For Circle dialogues, inward centering is essential. Reconnecting within, we touch the place in ourselves that can connect more meaningfully with others. We shift our focus from outer concerns to thoughts of the unseen forces in our lives—our quests for meaning and higher values, for heart-to-heart relating, for the common good, for community, for relatedness to the earth and nature, as well as for a more universal sense of moving in the web of life, connected to all that is. On all these levels, rituals open us to a spiritual experience of each other, so we can see beyond our outer forms and deeds to who we are and how we most want to be.

A good opening ceremony should therefore aim

- to create a good feeling of community and connection;
- to generate respect for others and for the anciently shared space of the Circle;

- to prepare people for releasing negative emotions in honest, respectful, and constructive ways;
- to open a safe space for the heart to speak and for mutual understanding to grow;
- to inspire participants to act on personal values;
- to reinforce shared values;
- to honor individual and collective capacities for rising to the Circle's call;
- to prepare participants to work together as a community; and
- to give a sense that the challenges each person faces are shared challenges best faced as a community.

Ceremonies that move people in these directions ideally reflect the culture and creativity of those involved. Such ceremonies may include saying prayers, reading poetry, dancing, listening to music, singing, lighting candles, meditating, storytelling, conscious breath work, sharing a time of silence, or sharing something of personal meaning in the Circle (pictures of ancestors or loved ones, a special poem, or a baseball glove used to play catch between successive generations of father and son). The Native American ritual of smudging—burning sage, sweetgrass, or other medicinal herbs which someone either places in the middle of the Circle or passes over participants, using a feather to move the smoke around them—allows people to cleanse themselves of negative energies and to prepare for sharing deeper emotions. Alice Lynch, Circle keeper and trainer and founder of BIHA (Black, Indian, Hispanic, and Asian Women in Action), describes the deeply spiritual focus of Circle ceremonies in many African American communities:

> The openings reflect our African American culture and so do the closings. Because we come from a strong spiritual

base, it is important that we have that reflected in everything we do. And I'm not speaking of religion, because
we do have multiple religious practices in our culture.
What I mean is that sometimes we might open with singing a religious song or just open with a prayer that reflects
our strong belief in a greater Being. In our culture, when
people are faced with controversy or difficult things,
they usually call on their Creator, whoever that might
be. That's the first place you turn, so in our community,
that's how we open our Circles.

Closing ceremonies

Closing ceremonies help people shift too. A good closing ceremony
allows people to digest the good that the Circle has achieved, honoring the wisdom, courage, and gifts of all participants. Closing
ceremonies reaffirm the connectedness that has developed and
express hope for the Circle's continued success. From the unique
atmosphere of the Circle, closing rituals also help participants shift
back to the regular pace of their lives.

The rituals used in the ceremonies can be simple or elaborate,
short or long. What's most important in designing them is their
capacity

- to respect all participants;
- to convey a sense of inclusiveness and connectedness;
- to appeal to personal values and the need to be guided
  by them;
- to open participants to their better selves; and
- to establish the Circle as a place of safety and respect.

Circle rituals are valuable not as ends in themselves but as
means of moving people closer to their spiritual center. If a ritual

does that, it's good. If not, it should be reexamined. The specific content isn't as important as the ritual's effectiveness in helping us connect to the values underlying Circles—to who we are in our heart's core and to our best sense of each other.

The Circle itself as a ceremony

Beyond the opening and closing ceremonies, the Circle itself is a ritual that communicates meaning. Sitting in the round says that everyone is included equally without regard to rank, status, or hierarchy. Shedding titles gives a further message of equality and of looking beyond outer roles to who we are in our hearts. Joining hands expresses community. The opening ceremony invites reflection and a spiritual sense of connectedness. The talking piece cultivates a capacity both to listen and to speak with respect. The guidelines convey shared ownership of the process and responsibility for its outcomes. And the closing ceremony inspires gratitude for the good achieved. Together, these rituals create a secure space where we can share personal stories, express emotions, be honest, take risks, and seek solutions to very difficult issues.

Contrasting the ceremonies of courts and Circles

In sentencing Circles in particular, the opening ritual serves not only to center and connect participants but also to distinguish the Circle from the court. Each process has its own purposes and distinct ways of responding to conflict. Specifically, court rituals send messages about the power and authority of the state. The judge sits above everyone else and must be addressed in certain ways. Everyone must rise when the judge enters or leaves. A bar or rail across the room separates lawyers from observers, further indicating detached authority. Special language and dress communicate who is important and who isn't. Inflexible rules say the law is more important than dealing with the unique needs and circumstances of a case. In these and many other ways, courts are designed ritually to concentrate power in state authority and then to use that coercive power to impose state "solutions" on social ills and human crises. Court rituals are all the more powerful because of their familiarity and cultural acceptance, which makes many of their messages about state authority functionally invisible.

Circles, by contrast, are designed to spread power equally and then to channel the shared power in peacemaking ways. In every detail, the rituals of Circles convey that we have within us the ability to work things out together in a good way. All we need is a respectful space and a process that supports the best in everyone.

Rituals are every bit as present and powerful today as they've always been in human culture. Today's rituals look different—rituals at the office that reinforce workplace roles or rituals at home that involve meals or watching television—but they are no less important in giving shape to our lives. Circles use the power of ritual and ceremony to support peacemaking processes. Circle ceremonies are designed to appeal to values, to cultivate meaningful relationships, to open possibilities for different ways of being together, and to invite constructive responses to conflict. Used carefully, Circle ceremonies provide a powerfully supportive framework for peacemaking dialogues.

Consensus-Based Decision-Making

The fifth element framing the Circle process is consensus—a much misunderstood concept. Consensus doesn't mean everyone necessarily agrees with the outcome as a first choice. It happens, but not often. Neither does it mean that one or both sides were forced to compromise. It's not an uncreative, piecemeal effort to bargain in order to achieve an outcome that no one finds satisfy-ing. Nor is it about passively submitting to the majority or politely agreeing when we really don't.

Incorporating all interests

Consensus is about being real—wholly real. It's about facing real situations in their totality, which means staying with complexity and not resorting to quick but partial or even one-sided decisions for relief. Consensus aims at whole-minded solutions that incor-porate everyone's interests as fully as possible. To generate such outcomes, participants don't keep a running checklist of who wants what and gets it; rather, they work together toward change that will be in everyone's best interests to help make happen. Realistically, this may not result in unanimity but rather in an agreement among all participants to "live with the outcome"—to accept a decision or course of action because it promises the best for everyone given the circumstances.

Circles encourage consensus, because they equip participants with the inner principles and values and the outer framework that make consensus logical and doable. Specifically, Circles give everyone an equal opportunity to speak and to be heard with respect. They also encourage careful listening, so that all interests go into generating the consensus. It's only natural, then, for Circles to call upon participants as a group to understand and integrate each person's interests in decisions. Everyone bears a responsibility in drawing in any interests that are not yet part of the consensus.

Not surprisingly, generating consensus involves tremendous patience, creativity, candor about interests and concerns, and a willingness to think outside the box. We're challenged to set aside our personal agendas and fixed notions about outcomes, so that something larger than any one person's preconceived ideas can emerge.

Creating new worlds

We could also say that consensus involves radically creative and holistic problem-solving, calling us to break through preset assumptions and expectations. Yet even that characterization doesn't capture it fully; "problem-solving" is too narrowly focused for what occurs. The deepest consensus involves creating new worlds where the original problems become less pressing, less relevant—worlds that include everyone and support their highest good equally.

This sounds off-the-charts idealistic, until we consider what consensus in Circles actually strives to achieve—and does achieve in many cases. For instance, in a tragically common situation, a drug-addicted young man steals for drugs and gets caught. However, instead of going to court, he is sent to a Circle. The "problem" to be solved is only superficially getting the youth to stop stealing. The greater problem is obviously the addiction. Yet here again, the "problem" is only superficially to get the young man to stop using drugs. The real solution lies in helping the young man claim his life—to create a world with the support of the community where he doesn't need to steal because he's not addicted, and he's not addicted because he's doing something with his life that gives him pride, joy, meaning, and self-worth. That's a world where his stealing and addiction don't exist anymore, a world that supports the highest good of everyone, and a world that everyone has good reason to join forces in creating.

Gaining a fuller awareness of differences

This is the kind of consensus that Circles seek. People can agree to a consensus, whether it's what they originally had in mind or not, if it makes sense to them to move in that direction. If it doesn't make sense, they shouldn't agree. If a proposed plan doesn't feel right to a participant, some important piece could be missing that could harm everyone, if not now, then down the road. The responsibility falls on dissenters to further articulate their concerns—not in a stonewalling way but in an open, exploring way—so that everyone can digest the issues raised and consider more options. And the responsibility falls on others to listen deeply to the dissenter's interests and to dig deeper or wider to find ways to encompass those interests. Circles don't dismiss or minimize differences, but they don't allow differences to become insurmountable barriers either. To build a consensus, we identify areas of disagreement and give them serious consideration, and then we use this fuller awareness of differences to make our final agreements more inclusive, hence stronger.

Dealing with deadlocks

A common objection to consensus is that lack of unanimity leads to deadlock and stymies action, causing the process to break down. Communities have responded to this challenge in different ways, especially in Circles called to design and run a Circle project. Within the spirit of consensus, communities are defining for themselves what consensus means and how to arrive there. For instance, one community dealing with environmental issues devised a process to work toward a consensus even when dissenting views remain unresolved. When a consensus isn't achieved at a meeting, the minority is asked to present their views again at the next meeting, and the majority has a specific responsibility to explore ways to include minority issues. If a consensus still can't be reached, the outstanding minority interests will be appended as part of the agreement, and the majority continues to look for ways to include the minority interests as the plan is implemented.

In a court process, those who prevail have no obligation to others; in a Circle, the desire to include all interests creates an ongoing commitment to seeking genuinely inclusive outcomes.

Unlike courts, Circles have the flexibility to devise methods that allow progress despite differences, but without railroading or ignoring minority concerns.

Applying Circle values to decision-making

This flexibility, combined with a strong focus on personal values and a capacity to evolve a shared vision, equips Circles to make decisions by consensus successfully. Indeed, consensus is the only decision-making method that's congruent with Circle values; namely, inclusivity and unconditional equality. Though forming a consensus takes time, skills, and patience that a top-down, hierarchical method doesn't require, the long-term outcome is far more practical. More interests and factors are woven into the decision. By respecting and including everyone equally in the process, consensus-based agreements generate comprehensive solutions. Whereas top-down decisions frequently create resentments, decisions achieved through consensus engage everyone, so everyone feels a responsibility for the outcome—for making the solution work.

A further evolution of democracy

The implications of consensus-based decision-making on our conception of democracy are profound. The modern Western notion of democracy accepts majority rule as the pinnacle of democratic self-government, as long as the minority has constitutional rights to protect them from majority abuse. Yet under this system, the same minority interests can be systematically ignored. Consensus decision-making goes the distance with democracy, striving to incorporate all interests in decisions. Kay reflects on the shift this triggered in her thinking:

It was Mark challenging me with questions about how we organize democratic representation and my experiences of working with consensus-based decision-making in Circles that prompted me to rethink democracy. Mark asked me, "Why do we define representation geographically? What if we had representation by interests?" I realized there was a potential for a further evolution of democracy, and that consensus is fundamentally more democratic than majority rule, because every interest must be attended to. No interest can be run over or swept aside. So this work has profoundly shifted my own personal sense of democracy.

These five fundamental elements—the keepers, the talking piece, the guidelines, the ceremonies, and the decision-making by consensus—provide the outer frame, or structure, for the Circle process. Again, the tree metaphor (see page 83) illustrates how these facets of Circles work together. First, the inner frame of Circles— the values, the principles, and the Medicine Wheel teaching of balance (chapter 2)—constitute the roots, the core philosophy that grounds Circles in a healing, constructive approach. Second, the outer basics of Circles—the five elements that we've considered in this chapter—constitute the trunk, the more visible frame that holds the Circle space. Third, what grows from the roots and trunk is the actual Circle process (the next two chapters), which brings healing, builds communities, and forms connections.

Chapter Four

How It All Comes Together: The Circle Process and Gathering

> *The most precious gift we can offer others is our presence.*
> *When mindfulness embraces those we love, they will*
> *bloom like flowers.*

—THICH NHAT HANH
Buddhist monk and peace activist

How do the inner and outer frames come together in the work of Circles? It's as if we've set up a room for a special kind of activity. What happens when we enter and start using it? What does the actual "doing" of Circles look like? In this chapter, we'll present a general overview of the Circle process and a Circle gathering. Though we have used the term "Circle process" rather broadly so far, for us the term technically refers to the multistage use of Circles in communities, distinct from "Circle," which refers to a particular gathering—people coming together for a specific purpose. Circles and the Circle process can be adapted to fit many different uses and serve a wide range of needs. In the next chapter, we'll describe how Circles can be adapted specifically for use in dealing with crimes.

AN OVERVIEW OF THE CIRCLE PROCESS

In sketching the "doing" of Circles, we don't intend to formalize them or to pin them down to some rigid or confining protocol. The Circle process is by nature messy, because humans and their conflicts are messy. Moreover, each process is different, because each case is unique. Were we to attempt to "clean it up" to make a Circle process fit a predetermined mold, we would straitjacket the process and restrict a Circle's potential to address the complexities that underlie a crime or conflict. David Hines, of Minnesota's Woodbury Police Department, describes Circles as being "an extremely fluid process." "They're not linear," he says, "they're called a 'circle' for a reason."

The four stages of the Circle process

With this fluid, open character of the Circle process in view, we can describe its four stages. Though each stage is crucial, the stages aren't fixed. They can assume different forms as well as be repeated or occur in various orders. These stages are

Stage 1. Determining suitability: Is the Circle the best process to use?

Stage 2. Preparation: How do the different parties need to prepare for coming together?

Stage 3. The peacemaking Circle—seeking a consensus agreement: When all consenting parties involved in a conflict are brought together in a Circle, how does it work? What process best meets the needs of everyone involved?

Stage 4. Follow-up and maintaining accountability: What happens next? Is arriving at an agreement the end as it is in courts, or is it a new beginning? How are agreements carried out, and what happens if someone breaks an agreement?

At each of these four stages, communities use differently focused Circles to work through the issues and to make decisions, as the diagram "Using Circles at Each Stage of the Process" illustrates.

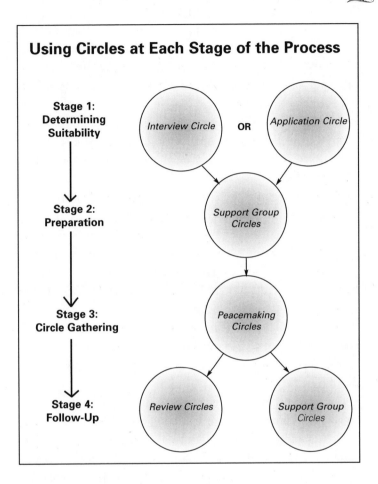

Using Circles at Each Stage of the Process

Stage 1:
Determining
Suitability

Interview Circle   OR   *Application Circle*

Stage 2:
Preparation

Support Group Circles

Stage 3:
Circle Gathering

Peacemaking Circles

Stage 4:
Follow-Up

Review Circles

Support Group Circles

The Circle gathering: an open and fluid process

Because Circles can be used at each stage, we will present an overview of how a Circle gathering works. Again, this is a proposed format for a Circle; it's not a formula for "how to do it right" nor a "to do" list for a keeper to check off.

In fact, for many Circles, some of the phases we name may not be relevant. The format we describe applies to Circles that deal with conflicts and crimes, but Circles can be adapted for many other purposes—support, understanding, learning, healing, finding harmony, community building, or simply celebrating being together. In these different types of Circles, the middle phases— what happens between the opening and the closing—will be entirely different, reflecting the Circle's purpose and responsive to the needs of those involved.

We emphasize this fluid, flexible, adaptive quality of Circles, because each Circle has its own wisdom and magic, as well as its unseen, healing logic for how best to unfold. Circles offer the possibility of uniting many hearts and minds as one, even if just for a moment. When and how this happens always has a touch of mystery to it. There's no formula for making an experience of one-mindedness, one-heartedness happen, any more than there's a formula for what makes us come alive, feel at peace, or take joy in feeling connected. Yet when these moments happen, they're gifts, inspiring hope that new ways of being together are possible.

Accordingly, what we describe in this section about Circle logistics and phases is simply a starting point for understanding a Circle gathering. Some things are essential, such as the wider conceptual framework—the Circle's values and principles, as well as the Medicine Wheel teaching of balance. Elements of the outer frame are essential too, such as the use of the talking piece, the guidelines, and making decisions by consensus. Without these pillars, we wouldn't experience a Circle's full potential. But what happens inside the Circle once these pillars are in place is entirely open.

The General Format of a Circle Gathering

Logistics: the physical dimension of a Circle

The logistics of a Circle gathering make up a large part of its physical dimension. For the Circle to be balanced, the care we invest in logistics is as important as the care we invest in the mental, emotional, and spiritual dimensions of the Circle process. Unfortunately, the physical aspects of a Circle often get short shrift. A Minneapolis keeper observed, "It's like how you want to prepare your home when people come to stay. You want them to feel comfortable, welcomed, and cared for—respected."

Communities have countless innovative ways of handling a Circle's physical side. Those who attend to minute details find that people notice. Participants feel immediately at ease—"like they really wanted me to be here and were real glad I came." Making the effort to deal with physical comforts starts the Circle in a good way and keeps people coming back. A Circle member commented, "You know, I'm only partly kidding when I say I keep coming to Circle because of the food and company that goes on here—you know what I'm saying."

Who takes responsibility for the logistics of a Circle varies with each community. Sometimes different people volunteer each time; other times the community justice coordinator assumes the overall responsibility.

The best location for a Circle is one that's accessible, quiet, peaceful, neutral, and perceived as belonging to the community. The chairs, preferably comfortable ones especially for Elders, are placed in a circle without a table in the middle. As we've mentioned, arranging chairs in the round conveys an atmosphere of equality as well as openness and receptivity. The chairs are set close enough to create a sense of connection. Some Circles leave one or two chairs open for latecomers, but most remove any empty chairs by the time the introductory round is completed. As much as possible, a space should be left behind the chairs for people to walk around outside the Circle.

Often a decorative cloth is placed in the middle with a candle on it. During preparation, keepers may invite participants to bring objects of significance to place on the cloth, which they can explain in the introductory round.

To promote a warm atmosphere and to ease anxieties, Circle committees make a point of greeting people as they enter, especially for the first time, and they often assign people to be greeters. Sometimes the entire group adopts this practice, which affirms everyone's role in sharing leadership and responsibility. Refreshments also create an easy, informal atmosphere, giving participants a chance to interact beforehand, on breaks, or after the Circle. People may also overlook the importance of what happens immediately following the Circle. When people linger over refreshments, keepers have a chance to informally thank people for coming, and this can be as important as welcoming them to the Circle.

Attending to these physical considerations makes participants feel welcomed and comfortable before, during, and after a Circle, and it has an enormous impact not just on the immediate Circle but also on keeping a community's support. Far from being insignificant or incidental, the informal spaces created around a Circle play an essential role in achieving *all* of the Circle's objectives, because they contribute to an atmosphere conducive to a respectful, cooperative endeavor.

The five phases of the Circle gathering

With the logistics in place, we can turn to the five phases of the Circle gathering. Again, these phases describe what generally goes on in Circles that deal with conflicts. Circles devoted to healing, support, community building, or understanding may not include all five phases. In Circles devoted to developing mutual under-standing, for instance, we listen to each other's different perspec-tives without expecting to arrive at a consensus. Circles honor differences and let them be. Only when some decision or action must be made does the issue of consensus arise. That said, the five phases of a Circle gathering include

Phase 1. Opening: creating the foundation for dialogue

Phase 2. Expressing needs and interests

Phase 3. Exploring options

Phase 4. Building consensus or a sense of unity

Phase 5. Closing: honoring the good achieved

Phase 1. Opening: creating the foundation for dialogue

The opening phase, essential to any Circle, generally has six parts:

    a. welcoming participants;
    b. sharing an opening ceremony;
    c. making introductions and doing a check-in;
    d. coming to a consensus about the guidelines;
    e. sharing a round of storytelling; and
    f. hearing the keeper's summary.

These six components assume many forms and occur in differ-ent orders, and not all are included in every opening. For example, regularly held Circles with the same participants may develop an understanding about the guidelines, so they may not need to dis-cuss them at every opening. So, too, the storytelling round may or may not serve a Circle's specific opening needs, or it may comprise the central body of a Circle. Whatever the opening, it's chosen for

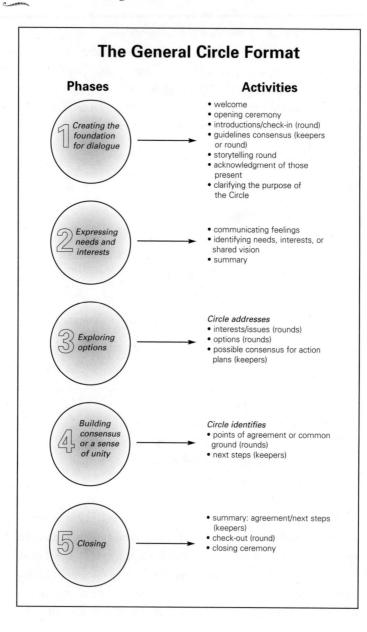

The General Circle Format

| **Phases** | **Activities** |

1 *Creating the foundation for dialogue*
- welcome
- opening ceremony
- introductions/check-in (round)
- guidelines consensus (keepers or round)
- storytelling round
- acknowledgment of those present
- clarifying the purpose of the Circle

2 *Expressing needs and interests*
- communicating feelings
- identifying needs, interests, or shared vision
- summary

3 *Exploring options*

Circle addresses
- interests/issues (rounds)
- options (rounds)
- possible consensus for action plans (keepers)

4 *Building consensus or a sense of unity*

Circle identifies
- points of agreement or common ground (rounds)
- next steps (keepers)

5 *Closing*
- summary: agreement/next steps (keepers)
- check-out (round)
- closing ceremony

its meaningful contribution to what the Circle is about. If done by rote, mechanically or unthinkingly, or from a sense of "should" or "ought to," the opening will be less engaging.

Openings are intended to help us shift our focus from our separateness to our relatedness. Good Circle openings invite us into a space where personal values count, where it's okay to express intense feelings, where spiritual experiences aren't dismissed, where seeking meaning in our lives matters, and where mutual respect, understanding, and trust are shared priorities. The opening is about moving us to a deeper place, and there are many ways to do this.

Keepers are responsible for the opening phase, but this responsibility calls for inviting others to plan and carry out different aspects of the opening. Sharing the opening sends a message that the Circle isn't the keepers' show but belongs to everyone.

Welcoming participants. The welcome sets the tone. Whoever does it thanks everyone for making the effort to be there. The welcome includes a brief description of the remaining parts of the opening phase. Keepers then explain the purpose of the opening ceremony—that it's a time for people to call upon their own sources of insight and guidance—and that no one is required to participate. They also explain how to use the talking piece. Finally, they reaffirm that after the introductions, the Circle will review all guidelines.

Opening ceremony. Next comes the opening ceremony, which moves people to a more reflective place. A keeper (or someone else) explains which ceremonies are proposed, what they mean, and why they're important, and then asks the Circle for permission to begin. Opening ceremonies are planned to include everyone. However, keepers encourage those who may feel uncomfortable to decline, assuring them that the Circle respects their wishes.

As we've discussed before, the opening ceremony can take many forms—perhaps a reading, a moment of meditation, or simply deep breathing. Whatever the form, the opening ceremony should reflect what has special meaning within the community. It should feel easy and natural, not weird, forced, or off-putting. Sometimes humor and lightness can be appropriate.

Opening ceremonies are often too brief and rushed—understandable but unfortunate. In the Circle process, the opening ceremony helps participants leave the scattered, hectic feel of everyday life and enter the sacred space of peacemaking. Designing ceremonies that do this effectively takes time. When two or more people share the privilege of planning it, the result tends to be richer in diversity and meets a broader range of needs.

Introductions and check-in. In the first round, the keepers ask participants to introduce themselves by sharing who they are, how they feel, and what they hope to achieve. In some Circles, people prefer to introduce themselves by their names or first names only rather than by their titles. This supports a sense of equality and encourages participants to see each other as people first instead of roles first. One or both keepers begin the round in order to model a deeper level of sharing—more from the heart about feelings and hopes and less about résumé-type information. If participants put meaningful objects in the middle of the Circle, this is a good time for explaining their significance. The introductory round gives everyone a sense of where people are emotionally and what's on their minds.

Seeking consensus around the guidelines is an essential part of the opening phase. Keepers review the basic Circle guidelines, raise any additional ones that have been suggested, and ask the Circle for further changes. Keepers may then pass the talking piece or hold it while they inquire if there are questions or suggestions. Though it takes time, a full round on the guidelines during the opening reaffirms the participatory nature of the process and demonstrates the importance of creating a safe and sacred space. Many ongoing Circles, such as those among the young people at Roca, review guidelines regularly as a way to revisit the values and principles on which their Circles depend. One keeper of a Circle dealing with the unintentional killing of a baby commented on the importance of spending time on the values and guidelines up front:

> After an opening reading and some calming breathing, I spoke a long time about the talking piece. I had the feeling that the talking piece was going to hold this Circle together—and it did. We each wrote a value on a plate and put the plates in the middle of the Circle. People referred several times to the values, as well as to their commitment to the talking piece and to hearing each other out. I spoke several times of people's patience—a value someone had laid out. On one occasion, someone said "I'm just glad I put 'self-control' in the middle there, because otherwise I wouldn't be using it."
>
> When things got rough, those guidelines and that talking piece formed the backup, the known limits, the comfort zone. People knew the guidelines and knew that these were necessary to keep this process moving forward. I have come to believe that the more overwhelming a Circle seems—the more pressed for time we feel to "get on with it"—the longer we should spend establishing values and guidelines. In this case, it was almost half an hour before we even got through guidelines. By then, everyone was breathing a little more deeply, and our mutual efforts had already begun the healing process.

A storytelling round. Inviting participants to share a personal life experience offers a powerful way to move beyond masks and appearances and to develop a better understanding of one another. Through storytelling, we find ourselves accessing wisdom from our own lives and using this wisdom to build bonds. We connect in ways that aren't directly related to the issue at hand. Sharing stories also supports a tone of speaking from our personal experiences, which lessens the urge to lecture. It expands our perspectives, elicits deep emotions, and spurs self-reflection without lapsing into one person telling another what to do. Most fundamentally, sharing our stories helps us experience each other as human beings, beyond how we may appear. Circle trainer Gwen Chandler-Rhivers recalls one story that brought this point home for her:

> In a Circle I'll always remember, there was a cop in the room. The cop had the reputation of being hard-nosed. Everybody backed away from the guy. You didn't talk to him, and you definitely didn't touch him.
>
> He started telling us his story about being one of thirteen children and living in the projects in Chicago. His dream for his family was that he would be the one to get his family out of the projects. So he told his story about playing football and how good he was at it. The hope and expectation was that he would get a scholarship. He got the scholarship to college and went to football training, but he didn't make the cut. That was the hardest phone call he ever made—to call his family and tell them, "I am not going to be the one."
>
> Now, every time he wakes up in the morning and puts on that policeman's uniform, he thinks about his family still in the projects in Chicago, and it's devastating for him. Every time he goes out into the community, that's the expression he wears on his face. When people meet him they think he's mean, angry, and bitter. In actuality, he is think-

ing about not being able to get his family out. He carries
this with him every day. But the perception others have of
him is something totally different. Once he was able to tell
his story, there wasn't a dry eye in the room.

For me, it just reinforces how you have to step back
from a situation and ask those hard questions. In this particular situation, he needed to tell his story, and we needed
to hear it. He wasn't being mean or angry; he was carrying
this awful burden. Being in that process with him helped
us to understand why we have to deal with each other as
human beings. We have to be in good relationship with
each other and not make assumptions about each other.
For that, we need to hear each other's stories.

As this case illustrates, sharing personal stories inspires trust by
helping us understand each other from the inside out. For those
who walk the often challenging path of peacemaking Circles, trust
is essential. When we open our hearts and lives to each other, we
create a safer environment for forming new relationships. These
relationships give us the strength to tackle the profound personal
and cultural change-work that Circles call us to do.

Sometimes we're not conscious of our stories, though. Serving
as a backdrop for our lives, they can become functionally invisible. Those who organize Circles find that we often need help with
coaxing our stories out into the open, and different activities may
support us in doing this. Don Johnson, a twenty-year prosecutor working in the juvenile justice system for Hennepin County,
Minnesota, as well as a national Circle trainer, uses many activities
to help people discover their stories:

We have different ways in which our stories have been
born in us, and no one of us carries just one story. To
access the different addresses of these stories inside us,

we need some creative expression that unlocks them. We need a key that fits each story and will let it flow out of us. It's as if we each have many doors inside, and each door requires a different key. The key to a particular door may be cognitive, but it may also be physical, intuitive, kinesthetic, emotional, or aesthetic. We may need to talk, but we may also need to paint, drum, dance, or sing. We need different ways of accessing ourselves to take full advantage of our stories, both to learn from our stories and to heal from them.

Keepers' summary. The keepers' summary closes the first phase and is crucial to setting the tone of the Circle. Drawing on what has been expressed in the check-in and storytelling rounds, keepers explain the context, clarifying the purpose of the Circle. They may also use the opportunity to share community news, to observe special personal events—births, birthdays, marriages, etc.—and to acknowledge progress in the lives of people in earlier Circles.

Starting Circle dialogue with building relationships. The opening phase doesn't deal directly with the issues that brought the Circle together. Indeed, it's essential *not* to start by talking about the issues. Circles first create a place that's emotionally safe for difficult exchanges by connecting people to each other. The stronger the relationships, the easier it'll be to work through differences.

Circle openings are designed to lay the ground for good relationships. Specifically, they help us connect with a more peaceful place within ourselves through the opening ceremonies. Participants experience what it's like to work together by coming to consensus on the guidelines. Circle openings also generate opportunities for sharing deeper sides of ourselves through the introduction, check-in, and storytelling. Quite intentionally, Circle openings start not by trying to solve something but by planting the seeds of community—by taking time to let people get to know each other and connect.

To convey the importance of taking the time to build relationships among participants, Harold Gatensby, a Tlingit First Nations Circle practitioner and teacher, identifies four components of the Circle inspired by the quadrants of the Medicine Wheel. These four components—getting acquainted, building understanding and trust, addressing issues or visions, and developing a plan of action—are equally important and so warrant relatively equal time. Anxious to get to the meat of the matter, people are often reluctant to take the time to get acquainted and build understanding and trust. Yet without trust, people may not speak their deepest truths about the issues. Consequently, any resulting plans don't work, lacking as they do a full awareness of what needs to be addressed. The temptation to move quickly through this relationship-building stage to the content part of the Circle undermines a Circle's potential. Kay reflects:

> This image is a powerful reminder for me to take the time for relationship-building when the pressure of the situation is pushing me to "get on with it." Participants in training sometimes express frustration with the time spent on things that don't feel productive to them. It creates tension for me, because I want to be responsive to the group, but I also want to be true to my own understanding of the Circle process. This Medicine Wheel image guides me in those situations.

After the opening phase, the Circle dialogue can jump back and forth through the next few phases, according to the unique needs and requirements of a situation. We've sorted out the Circle's dynamics into phases simply to name the different processes that

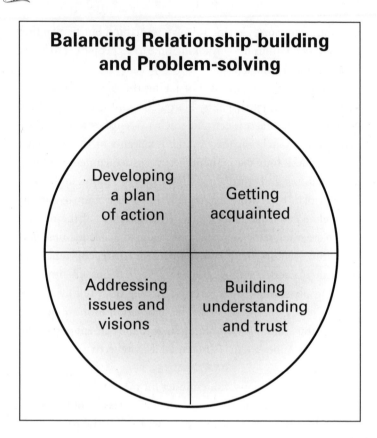

Balancing Relationship-building and Problem-solving

Developing a plan of action

Getting acquainted

Addressing issues and visions

Building understanding and trust

occur; in practice they flow together as participants work through problems.

Phase 2. Expressing needs and interests

Phase 2 begins with sharing information about what's happened, what has been done, and what people are experiencing. Its aim is to make sure everyone is working from a common base of information and is up-to-date on who's doing what. Phase 2 also gives people a chance to express feelings and concerns.

To provide the background, the keepers call on those with specific information to share. Once all the information is presented, participants respond. They express their feelings—their pain, anger, fear, confusions, and concerns—as well as their hopes for change. These rounds of the talking piece can elicit a wide range of emotions, and the problems may seem to get larger and more complex as people speak. This is natural, and keepers shouldn't try to move past this phase too quickly. The deep healing or whole-change processes that Circles generate requires that all concerns and feelings surface.

When the keepers sense that everyone's reactions have been thoroughly expressed, at least for the time being, they close this phase by acknowledging the emotions and restating the concerns raised. This is often a good time for a break.

Phase 3. Exploring options

Phase 3 expands the focus from what's gone wrong or what's hurting to what can be done to make things right, to promote healing, or to initiate positive change. In many Circles, such as those focused on support or healing, listening may be what's most needed—giving people a chance to tell their story and to have it received deeply. The move to "fix things" isn't always welcome or appropriate. Simply being heard may be the missing option that a person didn't have and wanted. In these situations, being heard can provide a sense of validation that is expansive and enables a person to move forward.

In other Circles, though, exploring options helps break the sense of being stuck in either a painful experience or a self-destructive way of life. Exploring options pushes back the walls that make change seem impossible. Because Circles include a diverse group of people, their capacity to generate options and find the means to carry them out is considerable. Circles can tap resources in the community that would be very hard for one person or one family to access.

During this phase, the search for constructive steps starts from the specific problem but rarely stays there. Circle dialogue seems naturally inclined to go beyond the immediate issue in two directions: (1) inward to participants' more personal stories, and (2) outward to the larger context or environment surrounding the crime. Both can shed light on the root of the problem and point to solutions.

Whereas the inward focus inspires change on personal and family levels, the outward focus acknowledges the social, economic, racial, political, educational, religious, ethnic, gender, and other collective dynamics that contribute to crime. The impetus in Circles to "get to the root of things" motivates us to complement immediate and obvious changes with more fundamental ones.

Both directions—inward and outward—help Circles generate creative options that address people's needs in sensitive and comprehensive ways.

Phase 4. Building consensus or a sense of unity

The fourth phase of the Circle gathering focuses on building a consensus: exploring the elements that may need to go into an agreement; clarifying what the consensus is; and devising a plan to carry it out. This phase is very important in Circles that, in the course of dealing with conflicts, must make decisions and plan actions. Yet not all Circles need to do this. Plenty of Circles have purposes that don't involve decisions or plans of action. The focus may be, for example, on understanding each other better, on learning, or on healing.

Even these Circles, though, often experience a version of this phase through a sense of unity. This unity isn't about everyone agreeing or being the same; it's about people coming together in an open, respectful way that doesn't treat differences as something that separates us. We can be different *and* feel a sense of unity, and Circles are conducive to this sense in a way that few public forums are.

When a decision must be made, Circles engage at this point in building a consensus. Weaving all the perspectives together in a process that respects everyone's contribution takes skill, care, and time. Parties with strong vested interests in the outcome can easily become locked in their positions or caught in their emotions, until they can't see their way to common ground. By creating the space for a community voice, Circles enable the community to be unbiased but caring "third parties." These third parties are able to absorb difficult sentiments and pose options that move both sides beyond entrenched positions.

For this reason, the consensus in most Circles evolves neither from one powerful voice nor from the key parties. Usually it's the community members who hold the space for a consensus to develop. They do this by respecting each point of view equally and by trying to understand the differences. Community members also introduce hopes and ideas about how to move forward. They create a more openly inquisitive, compassionate, and balanced atmosphere, which helps key players move beyond polarized positions. By expressing care and concern, community members create the space for people to explore a wider, more imaginative consensus.

Phase 5. Closing: valuing the good achieved

The closing of a Circle is as important as its opening, and it can have multiple parts as well. To close the gathering in a good way, the keepers review points of agreement and disagreement; participants share their final views and what they see as next steps; then the keepers initiate a closing round of reflection and introduce a closing ceremony.

The keepers summary. The keepers begin the closing process by summarizing what has emerged from the Circle. In doing this, they express gratitude for the contributions, patience, tolerance, cooperation, and time that everyone has invested in dealing with the issues in a good way.

The closing round. Next comes the closing round, in which keepers invite participants to speak not about the issues but about their experience of being in the Circle. Whatever emotions they may have experienced, they now have an opportunity to reflect on. Because this round shifts markedly from talking about issues to talking about everyone's inner experience of the Circle, the keepers often start to set the new tone, which involves some candor and vulnerability. After the round, the keepers can briefly acknowledge final concerns and once again thank everyone for contributing.

Though it's difficult to leave enough time for the closing round, it is very important to do so, because it invites everyone to step back and take a bigger view of what's occurred. Instead of letting Circles run to the agreed time limit and then begin the closing round, keepers need to allow thirty to forty minutes for this reflective sharing. In rare cases, keepers may ask whether participants would like to extend the Circle past the agreed-upon time.

The closing ceremony. The closing ceremony recognizes the efforts everyone has made to speak from the heart, to show respect and compassion for each other, and to create good relations. It helps participants make the transition from the unique space that Circles create to their everyday worlds where the interpersonal norm isn't generally as safe or open.

These five phases, like the chambers of a nautilus, hold the living, breathing experience of Circles. To convey this living sense, we'd like to share the following comments from participants about being in the Circle space:

> It was my first time to Circle, and the first time I've ever felt outside my family that there was a community of care. It made me cry. At first, I didn't know why I was crying. Now I do. I was crying because I was experiencing community. I was experiencing something I always wanted but was afraid to ask for. I never thought but always hoped to experience that sense of community.

> When the community was clearly just interested in supporting me—not because of what I might do for the offender—it helped me move beyond the pain I was feeling. I didn't want to be called or made out a victim. I was hurt. I needed help because I was hurting, not because I was a victim.

> One thing for sure, we need this Circle thing. This is the first time in twelve years at this plant that we've ever talked to each other. I mean really talked. This is the first time I'm getting to know people I've worked with for years. That cannot be a bad thing, and if it is, I say, let's have more bad things like this.

> I never have been included in anything in my community. It never seemed like I had anything to contribute. It always seemed that nothing anybody could do would

make a difference—yeah, same old, same old—but I could see in John's Circle that what I said got included. It felt good both then and after to see that I could contribute. I felt a part of my community in that Circle.

make a difference—yeah, same old, same old—but I
could see in John's Circle that what I said got included. It
felt good both then and after to see that I could contribute. I felt a part of my community in that Circle.

I started to say something else. I had it in my mind to say one thing, but something else came out. As it did, I was overwhelmed by emotions. At first, I was embarrassed by my tears, then I seemed to forget I was crying, because I felt so free, so good. I was reaching out to connect, not to help. You know, I wasn't asking for or giving help. I was just connecting—letting Susan and Henry know I understood. I respected and felt where they were and what had brought them to this place.

It's about the most sane process I've ever experienced.

Chapter Five

The Overall Circle Process
for Dealing with Crime

> *You go from feeling a heady responsibility as a Circle*
> *member. It's daunting. Then you remember that you*
> *only need to speak from the heart.*

—A VICTIM

> *The African American community has a lot of strength*
> *that we have not yet begun to tap.*

—JUDGE EDWARD WILSON
  Founding member of the Summit-University/Frogtown
  Community Circle, St. Paul, Minnesota

USING CIRCLES TO RESPOND TO CRIME isn't a single event. It's an ongoing process with stages that can extend over weeks, months, or years, depending on the case and the needs involved. The nature of the stages may change not only from community to community but also within a community from one case to the next. In setting out the stages of the overall Circle process for dealing with crime, we don't intend to prescribe a fixed method for how communities might use Circles. The Circle process is utterly flexible. We know of no formula for how a specific Circle process for a victim or offender "should" unfold—no automatic, assembly-line method that guarantees a predictable, uniform result.

Starting a community Circle initiative

Community Circle initiatives usually start with a few people who seek more healing and constructive ways to deal with crime in their families and neighborhoods. People of like mind come together and form the seed of a community justice committee (CJC). As word spreads and networking begins, people from various sectors of the community can be drawn to the project. With time, these committees may include people from all relevant agencies and sectors of the community, or they may be composed entirely of community volunteers.

In our experience, we have found that a mix of community volunteers and professionals—with the justice and other related agency representatives serving under the leadership of community volunteers—provides an effective balance for the peacemaking work. One public defender observed, "The community has to run the show. If lawyers are there, it is important for the community to be in charge." Ellen Barlow, a founding member of the St. Paul, Minnesota, Summit-University/Frogtown Community Circle, comments on how the Circle worked to establish community leadership:

> When we first started in 1998, we had to work hard to
> develop a relationship with the system people. We had
> to establish that the community was in charge, because
> there was so much distrust of the police and the system
> in our African American community. We took deliberate
> steps, like holding meetings within the community, to
> ensure that the procedure was really community driven
> and that everyone had an equal voice. We made sure that
> there wasn't the sense that the judges [Edward Wilson
> and Larry Cohen] were running it, even though they did
> come to us to get the Circle project started. It was really
> hard to make the transition from a system-driven to a
> community-driven process, because it took a lot of time
> to establish trust on all sides. Even the community members
> had to learn to trust each other.

The community justice committee supervises the overall Circle process and serves as a liaison with all those involved: with the court, law enforcement, treatment programs, and social service personnel, with other relevant agencies, as well as with all sectors of the community—families, schools, businesses, faith communities, nonprofits, and government representatives.

Establishing these relationships provides channels for cases to come into the Circle process. It also engages these sectors in supportive roles, so they're willing to serve as resources when needed. The more these relationships grow, the more the Circle initiative's success depends on the wider community's involvement and doesn't fall entirely on the shoulders of the committee and community members. Developing broader relationships also serves to keep the larger network informed about the progress of a specific case, so that rumors and misunderstandings are less likely to spread. And it builds trust in the process as problems are met through collaboration. Professionals come to embrace a sense of shared responsibility both from their roles as experts and authorities and from their lives as fellow community members. Not just the committee or the Circle participants but the far wider network becomes invested in making the process work. One St. Paul, Minnesota, community justice committee member said:

> To get the right fit for our community, we knew we had
> to get lots of people included. We're a community with
> lots of opinions about what works. We were not going
> to get the job done without at least trying to get a lot of
> people on board—and working with us.

Getting cases

Cases generally come to the community justice committee through the criminal justice system—referrals from the police, judges, or probation officers. Lawyers, especially public defenders, can also play active roles in referring cases. Other times victims or the offender's family might approach the committee for help. Again, building relationships, which involves education about restorative justice and the Circle process, establishes the means for cases to be referred.

In some communities—those where the Circle process is more widely understood—the community justice committee no longer depends on the justice system for referrals. Instead, Circle processes are initiated by an offender, victim, their families, or any community member. Although these cases begin without a commitment from the justice system to follow the Circle's decisions, the process proceeds as usual in supporting those most affected and in producing a recommended plan of action to the court. Insofar as the community Circle process involves a broad spectrum of community input, including justice professionals as community members, the judge often readily accepts the proposal. This approach involves far fewer formal justice resources in developing and carrying out a sentence. The more a Circle process is established in a community, so that people know about it and how it works, the more cases come by these means.

The four stages of the Circle process

However a case is referred, the community justice committee first decides whether the Circle process or some other restorative justice practice might be appropriate. This opens the first of the four stages we named in the previous chapter and which we will now consider at length in how they apply to dealing with crime. Again, these four stages are:

Stage 1. Determining suitability: Is the Circle the best process to use—both for the situation and for those involved? Other restorative justice practices, such as victim-offender mediation or family group conferencing, may serve the need better.

Stage 2. Preparation: What preparation do the different parties need before they come together? We have found that gathering all or some of the parties for a sentencing Circle requires extensive preparation for key participants. Without this, we jeopardize the potential of a sentencing Circle to be a positive experience, especially for victims.

Stage 3. The peacemaking Circle—seeking a consensus agreement for sentencing: When parties involved in a crime choose to come together in a Circle to decide how to repair the harm, what process can best meet the needs of everyone involved? Building on the work achieved in the previous stages, this stage develops a consensus—an agreement among all participants—that serves as a sentence.

Stage 4. Follow-up and maintaining accountability: What happens next? Is arriving at a sentence the end as it is in courts, or is it a new beginning? The effectiveness of Circles depends on everyone following through on agreements and continuing to support those in need. It also requires provisions for what to do if agreements are broken. The review Circles in this stage help to keep everyone, especially the offenders, on task. By doing so, they strengthen trust in the Circle process within both the community and the justice system.

STAGE 1. DETERMINING SUITABILITY: WHEN AND FOR WHOM ARE CIRCLES A GOOD CHOICE?

When we face a conflict of any kind, what process do we choose to respond? Our answer to this question is the first and most

important decision we make, because it determines the fundamental nature of the outcome. Specifically, the process we choose
profoundly affects

- *who* will participate;
- *how* they will participate;
- *what* values and interests will shape the outcomes;
- *what* information will be considered important, and
  when and if it will be presented;
- *whether* an agreement will be reached, *what* the agreement will contain, and *the degree of commitment* that
  participants invest in it to make it work;
- *whether* a conflict will be managed, settled, or resolved;
  and
- *what* shape and character relationships may take in the
  future.

Over the last thirty years, creative, constructive ways of resolving conflicts have become far more widely understood and prac-
ticed, offering many options besides the courts or other adversarial methods. For dealing with crime specifically, the emerging
field of community or restorative justice offers mediation, face-to-
face victim-offender meetings, family group conferencing, victim
panels, as well as Circles. Each process has its own distinct char-
acteristics, limits, strengths, and benefits. In an ideal community,
all these processes would be readily available.

To choose a process, those involved must first decide their
goals and which processes best serve those outcomes. Even then,
everyone must be flexible in responding to new information. As
we work through a crime or conflict, the nature of the problem,
how it can best be addressed, and who should be involved can
change dramatically.

For instance, when a young boy, Sam, threw a rock through

the window of a neighbor's car, the parties turned to mediation first to resolve the crime. Mediation uncovered child protection concerns: Sam's single mother, Helen, had a serious substance abuse problem and wasn't providing adequate parental care. When all parties decided to take the child protection case to a Circle, the process revealed that Helen was trafficking in drugs and that her neighbor, Sally, had been threatening to call the police. When Helen could neither find a job nor get help with her drug abuse, she began to take out her frustrations on Sam. In the month before the incident, she had become suicidal. As this information came to light, the process shifted first from mediation to a single Circle and then to multiple Circles: one for the child protection issue, one for the drug trafficking issue, and a healing and support Circle for Helen and Sam. Each process included different people, though with overlap. Sally, for example, became a strong supporter of both the son and his mother in the Circles.

In choosing a process to address the harm of crime, we need to remember that each situation is different and that no single process fits all crimes. The more practitioners are trained in different processes or practitioners of different processes work in fluid collaboration, the easier it will be to meet the shifting needs of a case.

When is a Circle a good process to use?

When choosing a process, we first need to consider the complexity of the situation: Do we want to get to the root of the problem and pursue the potential in this situation for wider change? Complex cases are best served by a process that's flexible and open-ended, one that focuses more on the process and less on the outcome. When we're single-mindedly focused on achieving a fixed outcome, we limit the process to the most obvious problem. Yet visible problems are often symptoms of deeper issues. Far more may need to be changed than appears on the surface, as in Sam's case.

Circles are an excellent choice for complex cases, since they're designed to be flexible and open-ended, hence capable of exploring all dimensions of a crime. They have the capacity to pursue conflicts to their roots and to rally the appropriate resources to effect fundamental changes. Circles use each crime as an opportunity for doing both curative and preventive work on relationships and communities. The curative work addresses the immediate harm or risk. The preventive work addresses the wider concerns, such as unresolved trauma, isolation, resource allocation, or institutional policies and practices that might be changed.

Besides complex situations, Circles are highly effective at dealing with harmful behavior that involves mixed responsibilities—situations with gray areas of culpability and no clear victim or offender, such as adolescent fights and bullying within schools. Such cases need a process that allows multiple perspectives to be aired and that's not structured around categorical labels for key participants. Circles are ideal for such situations.

Crimes among people in ongoing relationships—such as neighbors, family members, or classmates—present another type of situation where Circles may be a good choice. In such situations future contact is often likely between the parties. A process that addresses harm to the relationship and any underlying issues that may have contributed to the crime will make future contact more constructive and less likely to result in additional outbreaks of harmful conduct.

Theoretically, Circles can be used to prevent or resolve almost any problem, and anyone can call a Circle. The more participants understand the Circle process, the more effective the Circle can be. Once communities are experienced in Circles, they can call one whenever an issue arises. For example, a young couple who have been working with a community Circle for two years now grab the nearest object—a hairbrush, pen, or baby toy—to use as a talking piece for resolving their marital disputes.

Because Circles are so adaptable, it may be easier to determine Circle suitability, especially in formal justice cases, by considering why a Circle process might not work for a given situation. For example:

- *Lack of balance:* Can all interests involved in a conflict be included? Circles are designed to process imbalances. But to do this, Circles need all conflicting interests to be fairly and adequately represented. Since Circles work by consensus and not majority rule, they don't need equal numbers of conflicting parties to achieve balance, but they do need all views voiced in good faith. Circle training helps participants develop the value-based interaction that honors all sides of an issue, whether or not someone is present to voice a specific concern. If a potential Circle lacks a balanced representation, and if the Circle community has not been through a training to develop these skills, it isn't wise to proceed.
- *Lack of time:* Can those involved commit the time needed to do a Circle, which can be a long if not on-going process? Some cases can be resolved in one or two Circle gatherings, while other cases require ongoing support that may span months or years. Even if the process is relatively short, though, Circles entail a sub-stantial commitment from key participants, especially in criminal justice cases which require time for preparing the parties. How much time is needed depends on the people involved. Starting a Circle for any crime without the resolve to continue can be harmful to everyone. Simple problems that don't require a Circle can be settled more quickly through other means.
- *Capacity:* Are the resources available to do a Circle? To start, does the community have trained Circle

keepers and volunteer members who are willing to take on the case? Volunteers must commit not just to begin the process but also to see it through all four stages. Also, are the necessary professional resources involved? Although Circles can deal successfully with offenses such as sexual assault and spousal abuse, it's critical that appropriate resources for professional input and treatment are available. In such cases, victims' advocates need to be involved from beginning to end.

- *Safety:* Is the situation too volatile or dangerous? Safety issues might arise for victims, offenders, community members, or justice officials. Are the key players willing to commit to Circle principles both in and outside of Circles? If not, issues of safety and the danger of revictimizing victims may require a different choice of process, such as the courts. When safety is a concern but Circles seem to be the best process to use, an alternative may be to design one Circle for the victim and another for the offender.

- *Urgency:* Is there a deadline for a decision or some urgency about resolving a case? Circles can't guarantee a solution by a set date or time.

Deciding if a Circle process might suit an applicant

A community-based justice committee weighs all these factors and decides whether a Circle process is suitable for each case. Again, separate Circle processes may be needed for victims and offenders. The procedure for setting up a Circle for a victim is different from what we describe here. For offenders applying to the Circle process, either the full community justice committee or a subcommittee can process applications.

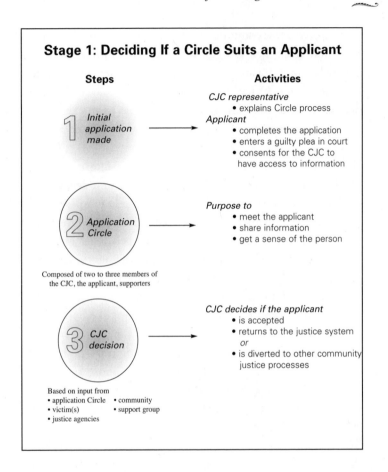

Stage 1: Deciding If a Circle Suits an Applicant

Steps	Activities

1 Initial application made

CJC representative
- explains Circle process

Applicant
- completes the application
- enters a guilty plea in court
- consents for the CJC to have access to information

2 Application Circle

Purpose to
- meet the applicant
- share information
- get a sense of the person

Composed of two to three members of
the CJC, the applicant, supporters

3 CJC decision

CJC decides if the applicant
- is accepted
- returns to the justice system
  or
- is diverted to other community justice processes

Based on input from
- application Circle
- victim(s)
- justice agencies
- community
- support group

To determine an applicant's suitability, community Circles typi-cally have application procedures, and they designate someone to answer all inquiries about the Circle process. To be considered for a Circle process, an applicant must first accept full responsibility for the crime and either enter a guilty plea in court or indicate a deci-sion to do so. He or she will then probably be asked to complete an application, participate in an application or interview Circle, gather a support group, and develop a plan for change.

Application. Most committees ask applicants to fill out a simple form indicating their charges, who their community supporters are, their reasons for applying to Circle, and a brief outline of their goals and plans. Often this application is completed through a one-on-one interview. The applicant must also permit the Circle's justice committee to have access to all relevant court documents.

Application or interview Circle. Based on the information supplied by the applicant and gathered from relevant agencies, the community justice committee convenes a Circle composed of the applicant, his or her support group, community volunteers, and professionals from the system (treatment personnel, probation officers, social workers, or police) to assess whether the case is appropriate for a Circle. To avoid overwhelming the applicant, some communities limit this Circle to three community people.

The application or interview Circle allows the applicant to experience the process, and it sets the tone for the relationship between the applicant and the Circle. The atmosphere should be one not of interrogation but of caring and support for someone who faces serious work in turning his or her life around. The gathering gives both the Circle members and the applicant a chance to learn about each other, hence the personal information shared should not be on the applicant's side alone. Neither should the information shared about the applicant be only negative. Application Circles explore the person's strengths, achievements, positive bonds, interests, and aspirations as well.

Before concluding, application Circles develop preliminary agreements for the applicant to see if the person can "walk the talk." They may adjourn both to gather additional information and to see how the applicant does in meeting the preliminary agreements. The application process may last a week or more than a month, depending on what the community justice committee decides is needed.

Criteria for deciding. Guidelines for acceptance vary according to the local design of the Circle project. The St. Paul, Minnesota, Summit-University/Frogtown Community Circle, for instance, focuses on African American offenders between the ages of eighteen and thirty-five who live or commit an offense in ward 1 and whose court sentence would normally include jail time. In general, exploring the suitability of an applicant involves

- reviewing all the written material available;
- meeting with the offender and supporters;
- reviewing the capabilities of the proposed support group;
- assessing the commitment of key participants;
- contacting key reference and referral sources; and
- consulting with the victim.

Considering all this information, the Circle decides by consensus whether to accept or reject the applicant. A decision to accept can be reviewed and reversed by consensus if the applicant fails to meet the conditions.

A Yukon community justice committee invites all applicants to attend their weekly meetings. Applicants can observe and participate in discussions about the suitability of other applicants. To be accepted for this particular Circle process, applicants must secure the support either of an Elder or of a diverse, committed support group. They must also accept responsibility for their crimes and demonstrate a commitment to change.

To decide whether an offender is suitable for the Circle, most communities consider the following factors:

1. The offender's attitude, input, and actions. The sooner an offender acknowledges responsibility and enters a guilty plea, the more likely he or she will be accepted into the Circle. Applicants who claim they're innocent or who express no remorse or will-ingness to change are not good candidates for the Circle process; they're best referred to the court.

If an applicant admits responsibility and expresses remorse, the committee must then assess whether the person is willing to commit to the Circle process, which includes attending Circle sessions, abiding by the agreements made in Circle, and engaging in the larger job of changing his or her life with the Circle's active support. Many young people in trouble have had to virtually fend for themselves all their lives. Having a roomful of people eager to help them—inquiring about their activities, making suggestions, and offering aid—can be disorienting and overwhelming. To help an offender, especially a juvenile, one or two volunteers may act as mentors and meet with the juvenile privately to help guide the youth through the Circle process.

2. The connection of the offender to the community. Supporting offenders through change as well as monitoring their behavior often depend on community involvement, and so the committee carefully considers the offender's community connections. The community may be geographic, institutional, or based on other connections.

Applicants need strong support groups—people who are com-mitted to helping the person through the demanding healing journey ahead. The support community may be drawn from the family, workplace, social or recreational spheres, church, or the neighborhood. If the applicant lacks a support group, one can be drawn from volunteers working for the community justice com-mittee and from relevant state agencies. Often the community Circle committee must search through the offender's personal network of family, friends, and associates as well as the larger com-munity to find willing support people. While many may volun-teer, few may be able to persevere through the inevitable setbacks.

Consequently, the Circle committee must monitor the support group to assess how they're doing and to determine whether the offender needs additional support to change his or her life.

3. The nature of the offense. In considering an application, most communities place more weight on the offender's circumstances than on the nature of the offense. A person charged with minor offenses may be accepted if the community believes the Circle can help to address significant personal or family issues. For example, a young girl was brought to a Circle for underage drinking, because the community recognized that both she and her family needed help. The minor offense opened the door for addressing much larger issues.

Some communities, however, decide to focus on specific kinds of offenders. For example, the Hollow Water community on Lake Winnipeg, Canada, deals exclusively with sex offenders; a Minnesota community deals only with spousal assaults; while another deals only with youth.

With serious offenses, the remedies will be different and may include jail, but the application procedure is essentially the same. In taking on offenders of serious crimes, communities must be sure they have the resources to meet the challenges of the case. Cases of addiction-related crimes and sex offenses, for instance, need treatment resources. "Quick fixes" are rarely possible, which means that communities need to be prepared to give long-term, consistent support. Though going the distance with these offenders is a daunting commitment, most communities believe that if they don't tackle serious offenses, significant changes in the community won't occur.

4. The views and interests of victims. In deciding whether to accept a case, the community justice committee solicits the views of victims. While victims usually don't have veto power, their views heavily influence the use of Circles. Being a voluntary process, Circles don't force victims to choose—either for themselves or for offenders—between the court process and the Circle. If a community accepts an offender into a Circle, victims have several options:

a. to participate in the Circle;
b. to participate in a Circle through a victim-services worker or other support person (some communities specifically invite people who have been victims of similar offenses to participate as supports);
c. to participate solely through the formal court (their testimony can be given in court and then related in the Circle);
d. to participate in a subsequent victim-offender reconciliation process; or
e. not to participate at all (Circle keepers or a victim-support worker can update victims on an offender's progress).

In addition to these options related to the offender's Circle process, victims may choose to participate in a support Circle of their own. The justice committee may rely on victim-support workers to ensure that everyone understands the victims' interests and that the victims choose freely whether and how to participate. Whatever their choice, the committee needs to keep the victim continually informed through the entire Circle process, unless he or she requests otherwise.

5. The views of other stakeholders. Any stakeholder who has an objection to an applicant's acceptance into a Circle is heard during the application process. Prosecutors, police, and probation officers are given opportunities to formally present any concerns they may have to the court and to the community. The community justice committee addresses the objections, exploring ways to meet the concerns. Once a Circle process is well established, the community and justice agencies develop partnerships that help them resolve their respective concerns.

Once again, the more justice personnel, especially police and prosecution, engage in Circles not just in their professional roles but also as community members, the more they understand Circles, respect them, and commit to the process. Once involved, formal justice players recognize the Circle's value not only to the community, offenders, and victims but also to their agencies' objectives. A Minneapolis prosecutor observed, "I didn't think the Circle would help us much. It seemed it might work for the offender and maybe in some cases benefit the community. But I must say I was surprised to find out how much the process and its results were totally in keeping with what my office policies were trying to achieve."

In turn, the community justice committee gains the help of justice professionals, who function more and more as resources and collaborators. A Minneapolis community justice committee member said, "Whatever else, the biggest change was our access to the judge and to many others who were so distant to us before. That new access makes such a big difference." A St. Paul Circle coordinator observed the same: "Just knowing I could call the prosecutor to talk about stuff that I didn't know was a great help to me."

Making plans for change. If the community justice committee or the full Circle accepts an applicant, the Circle urges the offender to develop a plan for making amends and working toward constructive personal change. When an offender shows recognition for the harm of his or her crime and wants to repair it, Circle participants are more motivated to commit themselves to the person's rehabilitation. These plans often become a part of the social compact between the offender and the Circle and eventually become a part of the actual sentence. Made in consensus with the applicant and his or her supporters, such plans might include having the applicant

- acknowledge the hurt caused to others;
- agree to be honest;
- commit in specific ways to healing and self-care;
- establish a balanced support group for guidance through the Circle process;
- identify a sponsor (a respected community member) who might chair the applicant's support group;
- meet as often as necessary with the Circle, support group, or its justice committee; and
- develop a plan for taking responsibility for the offense, which may include apologizing to, reconciling with, and in some way compensating all victims.

Besides coming up with a plan for the applicant, the Circle also details the responsibilities that supporters, community members, and criminal justice professionals will assume in supporting the individual as he or she works at making changes. In chapter 2, we described the case of Caroline and her mother, both of whom were selling drugs. The community had to find homes for each and support both through addiction treatment and the challenges of constructing new lives. In Circles, responsibilities are shared; they're not all on one side.

Taking time to weigh all the factors. Circles have no rigid formulas for determining whether an applicant is suitable for the process, since as far as we know, there's no perfect way to decide. Each community must choose its own process with an eye to keeping it simple and user friendly. Whatever process is used, though, taking time and care in determining Circle suitability—both for the particular situation and the applicant—pay off:

- It ensures that all parties enter the Circle process without false expectations and with a clear understanding of what the process involves.
- It identifies what special measures may be necessary to cover all interests.
- It explores other processes that might serve the situation better or that may supplement the Circle.
- And it makes necessary adjustments to the community Circle process to fit the distinct needs of a case.

There are also broader considerations. Whenever a new case arises, keepers as well as the justice committee need to pose some difficult questions about the Circle's capacity: Does the community have the resources to meet new commitments? Are there, for example, enough volunteers to take on new cases, given their current workload? Even with the best motives, overextending volunteer resources is risky, since volunteers can burn out. Equally problematic is taking on a case without the requisite professional resources. The Circle's justice committee needs to weigh all these factors—to consider what a new case might involve and to be realistic about what the Circle can and can't do. By taking time and care up front, the Circle can avoid accepting cases that might exhaust the community's resources or call for resources that the community simply doesn't have.

STAGE 2. PREPARING FOR THE SENTENCING CIRCLE

After an applicant has been accepted into the Circle process, the next step is to prepare all the parties who choose to participate, since the better the preparation, the better the Circle experience. Without adequate preparation, people may arrive anxious, fearful, confused, or shut down. The job of Circles becomes more difficult, and it takes longer to create a foundation for consensus. Good preparation brings the right people together to resolve conflict at its roots in the best way possible. What does this preparation involve? Six basic areas:

1. selecting keepers;
2. identifying essential people;
3. developing support groups;
4. formulating guidelines;
5. preparing ourselves; and
6. arranging preliminary Circles.

1. Selecting keepers

The community justice committee appoints two keepers as early as possible, since they handle most of the preparatory work. The keepers meet with key participants individually during the preparation stage, introducing themselves, their role, and the Circle process. They also arrange preliminary Circles as needed. Because of their contact with key participants at this early stage, keepers are the best monitors of what needs to be done and the best judges of when participants are ready to come together in a larger Circle.

For most people, Circles will be new. Keepers explain to participants how Circles work and let them know what's expected of them. This helps in a number of ways. It reduces participants' anxiety about entering a new situation, especially when they're already stressed from the crime and its aftermath. Further, the more participants know about Circles—the philosophy, principles, and values on which they're based—the more they can join in making the Circle environment constructive. Finally, understanding the process helps participants stay focused on the goal; namely, of bringing people together to share their truths and to seek a way forward that supports everyone's healing.

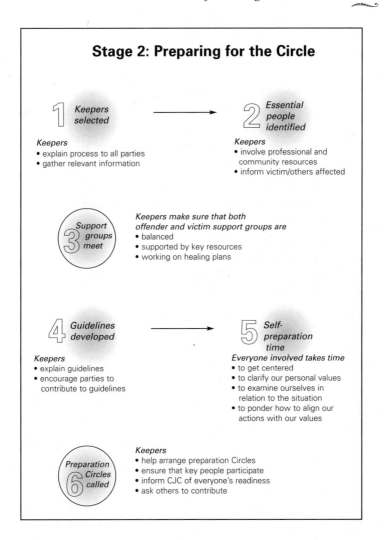

Stage 2: Preparing for the Circle

1 *Keepers selected*

Keepers
- explain process to all parties
- gather relevant information

2 *Essential people identified*

Keepers
- involve professional and community resources
- inform victim/others affected

3 *Support groups meet*

Keepers make sure that both offender and victim support groups are
- balanced
- supported by key resources
- working on healing plans

4 *Guidelines developed*

Keepers
- explain guidelines
- encourage parties to contribute to guidelines

5 *Self-preparation time*

Everyone involved takes time
- to get centered
- to clarify our personal values
- to examine ourselves in relation to the situation
- to ponder how to align our actions with our values

6 *Preparation Circles called*

Keepers
- help arrange preparation Circles
- ensure that key people participate
- inform CJC of everyone's readiness
- ask others to contribute

2. Identifying essential people

Preparation begins with determining who should be informed about and invited to participate in the Circle. Circles are open to the community, since every crime affects it. However, those directly involved in the case need to be contacted specifically. To identify these people, organizers and keepers need to consider:

- Who has been affected by the crime, and who is involved in responding to it?
- Who can provide support to those harmed?
- Who has resources or information that might be helpful?
- Who has significant relationships to the offender?
- Who has access to resources that would expand options for resolution?
- Who has relevant life experiences that could add insight (former addicts, ex-offenders, victims of similar crimes, families of offenders or victims, etc.)?

As the Circle process unfolds, keepers consider if any others should be invited.

3. Developing support groups

Few can recover from trauma, take risks, or develop new behavior patterns without caring, supportive relationships. These relationships may be with family, friends, colleagues, or neighbors, and the Circle committee can assist in developing these relationships. To avoid burning out community volunteers, support groups should include people outside the Circle committee. Finding good support people may take time, but it's worth the investment. Victims need support in reclaiming their personal power, and offenders need it for making long-term life changes. The success of the Circle process depends on support people to help sustain the momentum for healing beyond the Circle gatherings.

In exploring who might be part of a support group, keepers and the community justice committee ask such questions as:

Who is or has been important in your life? Who do you talk to about your problems? When you're in trouble, whom do you call for help?

Support people may come from unexpected places. A high school teacher, for example, joined a support group for someone who had been a student fifteen years earlier, while a union member came forward to support a former boss who was in a Circle to deal with his abusive conduct toward colleagues. Even strangers who volunteer can provide valuable support by adding fresh perspectives, by asking questions that cut through accepted or ignored behavior, and by demonstrating unqualified support. One offender spoke of a stranger in his support group:

> I didn't know her at all before. I hadn't even heard of her in the community, but what a difference she made. She was there for me not because she was paid, not because she was family, nor because she owed me something. She was there because, well, you know, I think because she just cared. Wow! She made me really think that if someone could give me that much support, I owed it back to her by giving it to anyone in my community.

Support people need to be willing to become involved in the applicant's life, both to offer help and to monitor how he or she is carrying out commitments made in the Circle. For applicants struggling to kick addictions, support people must be sober, stable, and reliable, and at least some of them should know from personal experience what lies ahead for the applicant on his or her healing journey.

In Yukon, ex-offenders who have traveled down the same self-destructive trail as the offender turn their "bad history into something good." Volunteering in a support group, an ex-offender came to appreciate "that all I went through can really help others. Doing that makes me feel like all those years, well, I haven't just wasted those years of my life. That wasted part can be used to help others. I can't tell you how much that helps me—by helping others."

For victims, the best practices and results flow from holding a separate support Circle to respect their interests. Communities may inadvertently be disrespectful to victims either by supporting an offender with a Circle but not holding one for the victim, or by holding a Circle for the victim mainly to secure a victim's input in the offender's Circle. Circles for victims should be held without pressuring the victim to participate in the offender's Circle. A Circle may still be valuable for the victim in cases where no one is charged with an offense or an offender pleads not guilty. Establishing a separate Circle for victims, no matter what an offender's circumstances, tells victims that the community recognizes their needs as equally important. Unlike the judicial system, Circles should not be primarily offender-driven; they must be driven equally (and at times separately) by the needs of victims and offenders as well as communities.

4. Formulating guidelines

Work on Circle guidelines also begins in the preparation stage. Keepers explain to participants how the six core guidelines assist in creating a safe place. Participants need to know the core guidelines before they come to the Circle. As we've said, keepers also invite participants to suggest additional guidelines that would help them participate in the Circle's dialogue.

5. Preparing ourselves

We can walk into a debate or discussion cold but not into a Circle. To engage in the spirit of dialogue, we need to prepare inwardly. Taking time to get centered, to clarify our personal values, and to think about how to align our conduct with our values helps us shift from a debate mind-set to one of dialogue. This is true for both keepers and participants, and self-preparation constitutes a vital and powerful piece of phase 2. Kay describes how she prepares herself for a Circle, whether she's keeping or participating:

> For me, there are two aspects of self-preparation. One is the specific preparation before going into a particular Circle. The other is the ongoing daily work of being mindful of acting on values and walking in the world in a way that is true to this worldview, so that it infuses everything.
>
> In preparation for a particular Circle, I try to find some time by myself and be very still and practice deep breathing. I call on the spirit helpers that I perceive to be in my life. I work on trying to release tension or negative energy. I do self-talk about being open and being clean, so that as a vessel for the energy that will flow in the Circle, I don't contaminate it.
>
> For my more general preparation, I rely heavily on a connection with nature to cleanse regularly, to be reminded of interconnectedness. Sometimes I think consciously about "walking gently on Mother Earth." Sometimes I seek the companionship of trees.
>
> This preparation helps to clear me, but it also helps me to realize that it's not about me—that I'm not working alone.

To help us find a more centered place relative to the specific issues or situation, we can ask ourselves some probing questions:

- What do I truly need from this process?
- Why do I feel I need these things?

- What actions will build trust, understanding, and respect for myself and others?
- What impact on myself and others will my actions have?
- How can I express my thoughts, feelings, needs, and concerns in a way that's respectful to myself and others?
- Can others accept or understand my actions and interests? Can I accept or understand theirs?
- What can I do to truly listen to others?
- What do I not understand about what others want?
- What can I do to encourage others to clarify what they need?
- Do I appreciate both what my actions mean to others and what their actions mean to them?

By posing these questions to ourselves, we become more aware of our own motives and needs as well as those of others, and this awareness prepares us to be in the Circle in a way that respects ourselves, our fellow participants, and the process.

6. Arranging preliminary Circles

Smaller Circles for various purposes (understanding, support, or healing) may be held separately for the victim and offender. Arranged by "invitation only," these Circles provide high levels of confidentiality and closeness. They don't try to fix problems but rather try to help those involved better understand the situation. They also provide support and caring. These Circles may explore a crime's impact, its underlying causes, options for amends or personal change, and potential resources. They try to give those in crisis a sense that they're not alone and a hope that constructive or healing outcomes are still possible.

Smaller Circles devoted to healing and understanding focus on the needs of a key player, and they can meet regularly for weeks or months to prepare those impacted by a crime for a joint gathering. It's not that the larger Circles can't handle and transform intense emotions. Rather, preparation Circles honor the needs of participants to go one step at a time and not to try to take on everything at once. They respect each person's timeline of self-awareness, healing, and transformation. They offer people the support of Circles without prematurely thrusting the most affected parties, especially victims, into emotionally charged situations. Sometimes one or both keepers will participate in these preparation Circles. Their participation helps assess who else needs to be involved and when the full Circle might be convened.

The benefits of good preparation

Nothing contributes to the success of a Circle more than careful preparation. Good preparation

- raises the comfort levels of participants by familiarizing them with the process beforehand;
- provides participants with information about the case as soon as possible, thereby preventing rumors and misinformation which could lead people to harden their positions;
- expedites access to support services, demonstrating a community's commitment to helping victims heal from wounds and helping offenders make personal changes;
- broadens the base of community participation, which increases the likelihood of the Circle's success;
- reduces the time needed in the full Circle;
- empowers vulnerable participants by ensuring their safety, giving them support, and enabling them to choose without pressure if and how they'll participate;

- helps participants clarify for themselves what they really need as an outcome, in contrast to what they may want from motives of "getting even," "hitting back," or avoiding responsibility by "getting off easy";
- develops everyone's peacemaking capacities; and
- introduces new ways of responding to pain and conflicts.

Clearly, preparation is essential. We underscore its role because of the common temptation, as Kay mentioned, to "get on with it" in dealing with a problem. Yet doing so would bypass the essence of Circles; namely, carefully nurturing people and relationships. Though over-preparation can also be a concern, bringing everyone together before they're ready can diminish a Circle's potential to generate innovative solutions. Knowing how much preparation different parties need is a judgment call for both keepers and participants. Given that there are no formulas and each case is different, keepers feel their way in gauging how much preparation is optimal.

STAGE 3. GATHERING ALL CONSENTING PARTIES IN A CIRCLE FOR SENTENCING

Adapting the four stages of the peacemaking Circle process to dealing with crime, this third stage brings together all the parties who choose to participate for the purpose of sentencing the offender. Sentencing in the Circle process is very different from sentencing in the courts. In the courts, arriving at a sentence is the main focus, the goal. When the sentence is passed, the job is done, and the court moves on to the next case.

In the Circle process, arriving at a sentence is a potentially healing experience—a journey of self-awareness and transformation. It's a time for expressing deep feelings, building relationships, and committing to a new beginning. It's also a time for offenders to build their self-esteem. They do this by holding themselves accountable for what they've done in constructive ways that enhance their sense of competence and autonomy.

When a Circle arrives at a sentence by a consensus process that includes the victim(s), the offender(s), families and friends, community members, and court professionals, everyone is to some extent changed through the process. Relationships are formed that will sustain victims and offenders through the months and possibly years to follow as the sentence is carried out.

The sentence itself represents a commitment by everyone involved in the consensus to build healthier lives and communities. A Circle sentence doesn't alienate or exile the applicant; it offers the means for his or her reintegration. Because so much more is involved in a Circle than in a court sentence, many Circles prefer the term "agreement," even though the agreement is later presented to the judge in court as the sentence.

When all the parties who agree to come together in a Circle feel they're ready, how does the Circle proceed in sentencing?

Logistical considerations specific to sentencing Circles

Again, the physical dimension of a Circle is exceedingly important, especially in dealing with the intense emotions surrounding crime. Care about physical, practical details communicates respect to all the participants, setting a respectful tone before the dialogue even begins. Naturally, the complexity and uniqueness of each crime carry implications for how the logistics are handled. For this reason, the keepers stay plugged into planning the logistics to make sure that the physical dimension as well as the parties' distinct needs and circumstances are handled appropriately. Every Circle will usually have something that requires special attention.

Because the work of Circles dealing with crimes, conflicts, and rebuilding people's lives is difficult, some physical arrangements help to create a supportive space for this particular use of Circles. For example, as the keeper mentioned earlier, some Circles write the values that they have named as important for coming together on paper plates and put them around the center for visual reminders. For the same purpose, Circle principles and guidelines may be posted on the walls. In Saskatoon, a courtroom has been specially designed for Circles. The room has the Medicine Wheel design in the carpet and the values set out in the four directions. "When you're in that room, you know you're in Circle and not in court."

Given the complexity of cases, the time needed for a Circle varies greatly. Ideally, it should be completely open. In indigenous communities, people talk and talk until "the real talk" begins, and no one knows how long that may take. For most people, though, their physical, mental, and emotional limit is three hours. After that time, instead of pressing on, it's usually better to adjourn and continue another time. Circles held in the evening or beginning at 4:00 P.M. seem to work well for many people's schedules.

To encourage attendance by community members and justice system professionals, Circle keepers and coordinators can post the time of each Circle and the case being addressed at locations that are readily accessible to the public. They can inform any relevant public and private organizations about a Circle gathering, as well as tell people with a direct interest in the case. By staying in close contact with key participants, keepers can ensure their attendance. A final reminder the day before the Circle allows keepers or coordinators to check in with them beforehand to address any unexpected concerns that may prevent their attending. As one Yukon keeper for a sentencing Circle observed:

> It is amazing. So often, the closer one gets to the time
> for Circle, the more stuff happens. It might just be last-
> minute jitters or whatever, but so many times, someone
> will hear something—or more often assume something—

and decide not to come. It's a good practice to check in with them, because all sorts of rumors fly just before Circle. I do. And several times if I hadn't, an important person for the Circle would not have been there because of a completely wrong assumption about something.

Given the emotions surrounding crime, seating warrants some attention as well. Some keepers sit beside each other, some sit opposite each other. The latter choice helps keepers balance the dialogue halfway through each round. In general, communities invite participants to sit where they're comfortable. Some communities have specific arrangements to advance both ceremonial aspects and safety. Victims and applicants sit next to someone in their support group. Defense counsel, if present, sits next to the applicant, and additional support people mix around the Circle.

Some communities have used an inner and outer Circle to accommodate large numbers. The key participants sit in the inner Circle. For the most part, those in the outer Circle serve as observers. During difficult times, though, they get the talking piece to help process intense emotions and work through issues. Though this can be a good arrangement for large numbers, we prefer to use one Circle and have done so for up to eighty people.

Countless other physical considerations may arise, and it's impossible to predict them. The point is to stay mindful of the supportive role that the physical dimension can have and to give it the time, energy, and attention it deserves.

The five phases of the Circle gathered for sentencing

Adapting Circles for sentencing involves special considerations. The Circle format is the same, but the purpose is to bring all interested parties together to work toward an appropriate, constructive sentence for the offender.

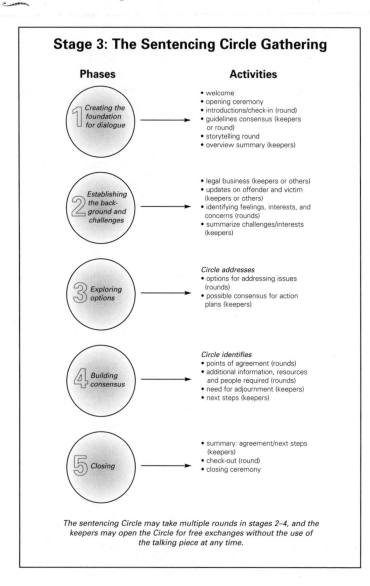

Stage 3: The Sentencing Circle Gathering

Phases	Activities

1 *Creating the foundation for dialogue*
- welcome
- opening ceremony
- introductions/check-in (round)
- guidelines consensus (keepers or round)
- storytelling round
- overview summary (keepers)

2 *Establishing the background and challenges*
- legal business (keepers or others)
- updates on offender and victim (keepers or others)
- identifying feelings, interests, and concerns (rounds)
- summarize challenges/interests (keepers)

3 *Exploring options*

Circle addresses
- options for addressing issues (rounds)
- possible consensus for action plans (keepers)

4 *Building consensus*

Circle identifies
- points of agreement (rounds)
- additional information, resources and people required (rounds)
- need for adjournment (keepers)
- next steps (keepers)

5 *Closing*
- summary: agreement/next steps (keepers)
- check-out (round)
- closing ceremony

The sentencing Circle may take multiple rounds in stages 2–4, and the keepers may open the Circle for free exchanges without the use of the talking piece at any time.

Phase 1. Creating the foundation for dialogue

The six parts of the opening phase—(a) welcoming participants; (b) sharing an opening ceremony; (c) making introductions and doing a check-in; (d) coming to a consensus about the guidelines; (e) sharing a round of storytelling; and (f) hearing the keeper's summary—each play a vital role in setting a positive tone for a sentencing Circle.

Welcoming participants. Besides the general welcoming comments, the welcome in sentencing Circles recognizes the Circle's contribution to the larger community. By sharing responsibility for the crime, the Circle enhances the lives of both individuals and the community on many levels. Keepers open with acknowledging this, so everyone appreciates the full importance of what they're striving to do.

After briefly describing the remaining parts of the opening phase, a sentencing Circle welcome reaffirms that after the introduction round, the Circle will review and seek a consensus about the guidelines.

Opening ceremony. Again, keepers invite different participants to offer the opening ceremony. The ceremonies vary immensely, but all have a similar purpose; namely, to help people shift to the Circle space. In Circles dealing with the effects of crime, the opening ceremony usually invites people to reflect on the interconnectedness of life and the need to respect the suffering of others—of victims, offenders, their families and friends, and the whole community.

Introductions and check-in. To avoid an attendance roll call as people introduce themselves, keepers can position people experienced in Circles next to them to model meaningful ways of self-introduction. Though the check-in round may take longer than expected, such unplanned processes deepen the connectedness among participants, which in turn makes future work easier.

Seeking consensus around the guidelines is an essential part of the opening phase, never more so than in a sentencing Circle. Working on the guidelines serves many functions. It follows through on the assurances that keepers gave participants during preparation that achieving an agreement on the guidelines helps to make the Circle a safe space, even for intense and painful emotions. Developing the guidelines together also underscores the collective responsibility for the quality of the Circle space and for the way participants conduct the dialogue. And it gives people a taste of what it's like to work toward common ground.

A storytelling round. In sentencing Circles, storytelling has proven time and again to be a powerful means of connection and transformation. Hearing others tell their life stories triggers memories of our own journeys. Instead of feeling isolated, we build bonds with others and feel supported by our common humanity—that we're not alone in our suffering, passions, mistakes, or joys. When Kathy, the older woman we mentioned earlier whose home was burglarized, heard the story of the young offender, fear-filled stereotypes gave way to a picture of a fellow human being, struggling through nightmarish histories of fear, neglect, abuse, and trauma. Through personal sharing, numbed emotions locked in pain gradually yield to care and empathy.

In a Circle for a young person, for example, people might be invited to share a story from their own youth when they were in conflict with their parents, when they felt excluded, or when they faced a situation they didn't know how to handle. Sharing such experiences is likely to make the young person feel understood and treated with compassion. For those in grief or trauma, sharing painful experiences and being heard with respect brings balm to wounds and validates their suffering. Storytelling helps us find ourselves in each other, reducing the distance we may feel from one another by discovering common ground.

Storytelling also frames the Circle dialogue around expressions of direct personal experiences. Instead of quoting legal precedents, contesting facts, arguing technical points, passing judgments, or lecturing, participants speak from their hearts about their own life lessons. Dr. Thomas Angelo, a specialist in teaching and learning, commented, "Stories are the best way of organizing information. It is true for all cultures I know." Stories give us a better understanding of people and situations, because they provide a context for information that's understandable; namely, life experiences. Identifying with another's personal struggles, we shift to a more compassionate frame of mind and move away from an adversarial, us-them tone.

Finally, personal stories inspire hope. As community Circles develop over time, former offenders tell newcomers their stories of transformation, and former victims share their experiences of healing with those still raw with grief and despairing of life beyond the traumatic event. These stories offer a vision of our human capacities for renewal and growth.

Keepers' summary. Principally, the keepers' summary describes the overall challenges facing the Circle. The emphasis, though, is less on specifics and more on expressing confidence in everyone's commitment to finding common ground and to working things out in a good way. By showing up, participants take an important first step toward the joint search for solutions.

Starting Circle dialogue with building relationships. As with all Circles, the aim in a sentencing Circle—reflected in the nonissue content of the opening—isn't just to pass a sentence but far more to build or rebuild relationships. Recognizing each person's values, perspectives, and circumstances provides a better start to a difficult dialogue about crime than focusing on the facts of a case. Starting with facts can trigger highly emotional responses. It can further divide participants into the categories of victims, victim supporters, offender, offender supporters, or professionals, and then it can induce participants to stake out positions before they have gained a sense of others as people.

Circles open difficult conversations by focusing on the people involved: appreciating that they all belong to a community, identifying how they're connected, and exploring their shared values and objectives. Participants learn about each other as individuals. In the process, they feel respected and empowered by being heard. No matter what issues a Circle faces, participants find it easier to deal with them constructively when they first gain a sense of each other as people.

Phase 2. Establishing the legal background and identifying challenges

After the opening, the next step is to present the facts and name the challenges. This phase generally includes three parts:

a. handling the legal business and giving updates;
b. identifying concerns, issues, and interests; and
c. hearing the keepers' summary.

Legal business and update. In the sentencing Circle, phase 2 begins with the "legal business." If a judge is present, he or she may lead this part in much the same order as sentencing occurs in court. The prosecutor reads the facts establishing the charges. When the applicant accepts the facts, a guilty plea is formally accepted in the Circle. It's important for everyone to know the facts of the crime and to see the applicant taking full responsibility. The prosecutor and defense counsel may be called upon to make brief opening statements. Any key information—e.g., a criminal record, presentence report, or victim impact statement—is shared and, if need be, passed around the Circle. A probation officer may summarize his or her report. The judge may finish the legal business by briefly stating what the sentence might be in court, voicing any concerns, and expressing appreciation to the community and others in working together to find the best means of addressing all concerns. Sometimes judges sense a need to remind the Circle that the outcome will be based on a consensus and that the judge's input is only one voice. This reminds everyone to direct their comments to the Circle, not the judge.

In sentencing Circles where no judge, prosecutor, defense counsel, or probation officer is present, the keepers may handle the legal business themselves or ask someone else to do it. However, most community justice committees develop enough positive relationships with justice and law enforcement professionals to have at least some of them participating in the Circle, either as visiting professionals or as regular community members. Their involvement is important to cultivate, since they possess unique experience in dealing with offenders.

A keeper or other informed person then tells the Circle the case's status, including an update on the victim and the offender. Having consulted beforehand with the support groups and others to see if they're willing to share information, keepers ask them to brief the Circle. When it's time for these updates, the keeper may hold the talking piece, ask the Circle to pass it to each person who is to speak, or walk the talking piece to whoever is providing background and legal facts. In some Circles, the applicant and victim then make their first input. However, most Circles rely on the rounds of the talking piece to bring out their voices when they're ready.

In other words, phase 2 establishes a common base of information, so everyone knows the current status of where things stand and who's doing what. Even small steps toward personal change can be worth mentioning during this time, since these can fuel a positive momentum within the Circle.

Identifying concerns, issues, and interests. Once all the information is presented, the keepers may begin a round by acknowledging the challenges facing the Circle and then passing the talking piece for others to respond. During the rounds of sharing that follow, keepers can underscore the importance of being open and honest—of stating candidly what's on people's minds, as long as it's done from the heart. Hard feelings need to be expressed, so that the Circle knows the full picture—not only factually but also emotionally. As people speak from what they feel, they find they're able to express their feelings respectfully, not hurtfully. They might say, for example, "This hurt me so much, I can't sleep, I don't feel safe, I'm angry and afraid, and now I have feelings of wanting revenge; I don't want to live this way." If shared openly in Circle, such difficult emotions—and the complex problems that go with them—are not barriers but rather the essential ingredients for creating realistic, sustainable outcomes.

The keepers' summary. When everyone has expressed their feelings and concerns as much as they want or are able to do at this point, keepers close this phase by acknowledging the feelings shared, restating the concerns raised, and thanking everyone for their contributions and courage.

If the first two phases have taken a long time, a break may be in order. Breaks offer support groups a chance to process what has happened, raise any outstanding concerns, and consider options. Breaks also give keepers a chance to check privately with key participants to see how they're doing and if they have any concerns.

Phase 3. Exploring options for sentencing

In the third phase, participants explore options for sentencing and develop action plans. Keepers begin this round by building on ideas already shared and asking the Circle for other suggestions on addressing concerns and the harm surrounding the crime. After a round, the keepers may hold the talking piece and open the Circle for spontaneous discussion. They might also initiate a round by asking participants what they each might do to help address the issues. The keepers can "park" the options generated on a flip chart to make sure none are forgotten.

In our experience, communities are creative, sensitive, and constructive in developing sentencing options. Unlike court sentences, Circle sentences have no intention to inflict harm or suffering in equal or comparable measure. Their goal is positive personal change, not punishment. To this end, Circle sentences focus on three areas:

a. repairing harm to the victim in whatever way possible;
b. making amends to the community; and
c. addressing the underlying causes, so that further crimes are less likely to happen.

From her experience with a Circle initiative devoted to helping African American young men stay out of prison by changing their lives, Gwen Chandler-Rhivers gives an example:

> Communities are able to be creative in determining sentences. They first look at the impact that the crime has had on them and then think of ways to repair that harm. The first case we had involved a young man who had been convicted of dealing crack cocaine and had a new offense of carrying a firearm. Part of his sentence was to

do community service hours in the local hospital rock-
ing crack-addicted babies. The other community service
hours were spent as a personal-care attendant for a gun-
shot victim. This type of creative sentencing dealt with
both criminal offenses.

Naturally, such solutions require the community and the offender to spend time working together. "One of the things about
sentencing that people sometimes get confused about," Gwen
Chandler-Rhivers notes, "is that sentencing doesn't take place until
the community and the offender feel as if they're ready—meaning
that the offender has made some significant gains and has taken
steps toward repairing the harm that he or she has caused."

Drawing on everyone's input, the keepers may summarize the
points of agreement, remaining issues, and the positive potential
they see emerging, taking care to respect all contributions and to
avoid favoring any one sentencing option. It's the Circle's job and
not the keepers' to sift through the ideas. While generating options, people may realize that they need more information, and
the keepers may focus the Circle on figuring out how to get it. In
summarizing the third phase, keepers acknowledge the hard work
and positive efforts of the group.

Phase 4. *Building consensus for a sentencing agreement*

Building consensus for a sentence takes time. Again, some cases
may require weeks or months to work out a sentence, while others
may require only one session.

When a case turns out to be difficult or complex, allowing the
process to extend over time can help. Taking time off—either
short periods through breaks or longer periods through adjournments—can actually move the Circle toward consensus. Breaks
allow everyone to step back and discuss things privately; discus-

sions between keepers and participants can be especially productive. On reconvening, people can pose difficulties for the Circle to address.

Adjourning for a few weeks or months also has advantages. First, everyone has time to consider the options raised in the Circle and to gather more information. Second, adjourning gives key participants a chance to prove their resolve by meeting their preliminary commitments and by making changes in good faith. Circle participants may not disagree with a proposed consensus agreement, but they may have doubts about whether the offender can carry it out. Giving offenders time to "walk their talk" frequently removes these objections. Third, adjournment gives the community and agency professionals time to follow through on the promises they made in Circle as well. Finally, adjournment gives everyone a chance to catch up with what happened, both emotionally and mentally. Circles can generate changes that take time to absorb and accept. One victim supporter noted:

> I needed time to catch up with what happened in the
> Circle both mentally and emotionally. I felt the need to
> see things differently, but I needed time to make sure I
> was really ready—ready to accept the changes I felt were
> right to make.

If consensus on a sentence has been reached. In a Circle where a consensus has been reached but there's not enough time to figure out the details, keepers outline the main points and ask everyone to think of what can be done to strengthen or improve the consensus. The Circle then adjourns after arranging to reconvene to work out a plan for implementing the agreement. Holding a separate Circle to clarify the consensus and how it will work helps to prevent confusion, false assumptions, and negative speculations.

Everyone leaves the clarifying Circle with the same understanding. Without thorough clarification, misunderstandings about who does what or what happens when can severely damage the consensus.

For example, when Dick thought he would be fully reunited with his family after completing a residential addiction treatment program, and others thought the reunion would be phased in gradually, serious problems arose when he moved back with his family right after treatment. The community members believed Dick ignored his commitment. He believed the community was unfairly making new demands and not sufficiently recognizing his hard-won progress in treatment.

Because misunderstandings like this can happen so easily, the task of clarifying a consensus warrants time, if not a separate Circle. Moreover, as with adjournments on the way to a consensus, the adjournment between the Circle that made the consensus and the one devoted to clarifying it offers additional advantages.

First, it gives the new world of the consensus a chance to settle in. We have an opportunity to step back, assess what's been achieved, and consider all the implications. In one case, the initial agreement hadn't accounted for what would happen to an offender's two young sons each weekend while he was attending a residential treatment program. When the Circle met to clarify the agreement, two families, both of whom had children the same ages, offered to include his sons each weekend in their outings.

Second, the time in adjournment encourages participants not only to work out the details but also to consider how to improve an agreement. Coming to a consensus can be so difficult that when it's finally achieved, we want to grab it and run. If we do, though, we miss countless openings for creating something even better. Reaching a consensus introduces a new world. After it has been achieved, exploring even broader, more inclusive agreements becomes easier, since the fallback position is an agreement. The consensus also fosters a new environment of trust and a desire to solve problems rather than merely advance personal positions. Many golden opportunities can be left on the table when parties to a new agreement don't pause long enough to entertain potential improvements.

A judge, for example, offered to write a letter of support to prospective employers on behalf of Mary, an offender, if she kept her commitments to the Circle. She in turn offered to teach the young women in the community to sew if she found a job that allowed her to buy a sewing machine. That promise inspired someone to let Mary use her sewing machine and to offer a room for her to teach sewing classes. And so it went. When we struggle through our differences and finally gain consensus, what can grow from the new ground is amazing—that is, if we take the time to cultivate its possibilities.

Third, we can use the adjournment to write out the consensus from all angles. In a Circle consensus, the offender isn't the only one who has obligations. All the participants—the offender, the family, friends, supporters, community members, and state agency personnel—have roles to play and tasks to fulfill. A Circle consensus reflects the holistic idea that it "takes a village" to make significant, sustained change. Because of the complexities—who does what when, with whom, and under which circumstances—these obligations are best expressed not just through prose but also through graphic illustrations, diagrams, or flow charts. For instance, drawing overlapping circles—each containing the commitments of the offender, community members, and state agency personnel—can depict visually the contributions that each person has agreed to make.

By the end of a sentencing Circle that has reached a consensus, people may be too rushed or tired to write out the agreement. If so, it's best to adjourn and designate someone to produce a draft as soon as possible. Keepers are a logical choice to do this. They can ask key participants to check the draft for accuracy before the next Circle, when the group can either finalize the agreement or continue to work on it.

When the Circle reconvenes after a period of adjournment, the keepers begin to clarify the consensus by asking the Circle whether

- all interests have been addressed;
- all the resources needed to carry out the plan, including funds, are available;
- all the people and agencies who must cooperate to make the plan work are on board;
- the timing of jobs, duties, commitments, and events are spelled out;
- the goals, objectives and deadlines are realistic and doable;
- provisions are made for delays, violations, or unforeseen events, so everyone knows the procedure for revising the plan; and
- participants are aware of what might happen if commitments are honored and what might happen if they're not.

Besides making sure that the consensus agreement (sentence) is simple, realistic, fair, and inclusive, keepers call on the Circle to provide safety nets to catch falls from the high wire of Circle-made commitments. These safety nets can take many forms—e.g., monitoring, reviews, and an agreement to return to the Circle when any difficulties arise. Safety nets can also develop from several "follow-up" features of the sentence:

- *Clearly stated, enforceable commitments.* What's expected of each person? When, where, and how will people

carry out their consensus-defined commitments?
Clarifying everyone's responsibilities makes it easier to
put the agreement into practice and monitor how it's
working.

- *Clearly expressed outcomes.* What do success and failure
  mean? What happens if agreements aren't kept? Failing
  to set consequences for agreement violations undermines community and justice system confidence in
  Circles and jeopardizes the Circle's funding. Moreover,
  when an offender fails to honor commitments and
  nothing is done, the community or state agencies
  become less willing to offer similar chances to others.
  Offenders need to realize that their conduct affects
  not only their own chances for a new life but also the
  opportunities of those who follow them.

  The consequences of success are equally important to spell out. For offenders, success may mean
  no further sanctions from the state. For both victims
  and offenders, it may mean a community's commitment to help with housing, employment, day care, or
  counseling. Success may, in fact, mean any number of
  ways that families or a community can contribute to a
  person's progress along the arduous road of recovery.

- *Handling violations of the agreement.* The plan for implementing the agreement must be both flexible and
  realistic. We have found that rigid responses to violations of the agreement are not the best route. Circles
  have the capacity to deal with them differently. They
  can do the hard work of appreciating the full context
  of the violation—why it happened and what triggered it. They can give offenders a chance to account
  for their behavior, and then they can work with them
  to deal with the issues, whatever they are. When, for

example, Jane relapsed to an addiction and failed once again to return home to take care of her child, she was not marched off to jail. Jane had achieved her first two months of sobriety in years. She relapsed after another job interview went sour. Her child was taken. Jane spent another week in relapse, but after that week, the community helped her find a part-time job, and she got back into recovery. People who have struggled for years with substance abuse will suffer relapse. Addiction counselors know this, and communities must learn how to help recovering addicts through these periods, since relapses are common during the healing process.

In short, if a consensus on a sentence has been reached, taking time to clarify it honors the Circle's achievement. It provides insurance for the journey that the consensus charts into the uncertain waters of the future. Everyone has a stake in the journey's success, since it carries hope for fundamental changes. The consensus clears the way for the Circle's most important work: transforming hopes and dreams into realities.

If a consensus has not been reached. A Circle may not reach a consensus in all cases, regardless of how hard they try or how many sessions they work at it. When this happens, the judge, based on all the input from the Circle, will decide the sentence. If the judge has been present throughout, this decision is best rendered in the Circle. If the Circle has proceeded without a judge, the points of agreement and disagreement can be presented as part of the sentencing process. Whatever consensus was achieved gets incorporated into the judge's decision, which draws strongly on the Circle's input. In our experience, though, being unable to reach consensus on a sentence is rare, especially if Circles give offenders time to "walk their talk" and prove their commitment.

In other words, even when a Circle can't reach a consensus, the time and effort put into it aren't lost. Not only does the Circle process help participants understand the broader implications of a crime, but it also produces a more insightful sentence. "The few times we failed to reach a consensus," a judge commented, "the sentencing [in court] was easier and much more effective. This wasn't just because of the education we all gained from the process, but also because we got to know so much more about the offender, victim, and community. The sentence was able to focus on primary issues."

Phase 5. Closing: honoring the efforts made

Whether or not a particular Circle has reached consensus, the very process of engaging in the Circle is worth celebrating, which is what the closing phase is designed to do. Sharing the struggle to find resolution, having the courage to speak openly and honestly, showing respect when emotions are hot, persevering through frustration and deadlock, maintaining trust in the Circle process, which ultimately means keeping faith in ourselves and each other: all these efforts help participants better understand one another, improve relationships, and strengthen the community. In most cases, these are the most important outcomes of Circles. Good work is done whether or not consensus follows. The closing phase acknowledges all the efforts made and the good achieved.

The keepers summary. The keepers begin the closing process by summarizing the agreement and disagreement that emerged during the sentencing process. They may even use another round of the talking piece to check everyone's views and make sure that they've mentioned all the relevant points. The keepers then review what everyone has agreed to do in the next steps. Again, they express gratitude for all the efforts made to deal with the issues and each other in a respectful, honest, and open way.

The closing round. Keepers usually begin this round so they can model the shift from talking about issues to reflecting on the personal experience of being in the Circle. By inviting people to share what they felt during the process, the closing round can have a humanizing, equalizing effect. It's not about positions or roles; it's about people coming together to help change lives. This is profound work, whatever role one plays in it, and the closing round honors the time shared in transformation and healing.

The closing ceremony. The closing ceremony for a sentencing Circle celebrates what has been accomplished in whatever way feels most appropriate and meaningful for those involved. Given the unpredictable nature of such Circles, closing ceremonies may be difficult to plan. Sometimes impromptu words by those who feel moved best fits the occasion. Whatever form the closing ceremony may take, it sends people off to their individual lives appreciating what can happen when people come together to work through some of the hardest experiences in life in a good way.

To convey what it's like to experience a sentencing Circle gathering, we'll share some comments made by victims, offenders, community members, and justice professionals. One victim, for example, made this observation about her first sentencing Circle gathering:

> I didn't expect [the offender] to apologize, even though
> I was told he would. I also didn't expect it would change
> so much for me. Even more surprising for me was how

much it meant for his family to apologize and accept responsibility. I could really feel the difference.

A member of a victim's family said:

> I came here hating them. I didn't really want to come. I
> was so sick of it all. It was hurting me so much, I wanted
> to hurt back. Sometimes I was angry enough to hurt
> them. Sometimes I was so down, I could have hurt my-
> self. I don't know how I got here, but I thank the Creator
> and Jean [a support woman] for getting me here. I'm
> leaving here without anger. I hope soon to be able to
> forgive the people here—all of you—including those I
> came here to hate and to hurt. So many people here have
> made it possible for me to leave in a better way. All of us
> took risks. I do thank those who cried and shared their
> pain. I felt it and shared it. I give thanks to all who heard
> my pain. I feel it was shared, even felt, by others. We have
> certainly begun to feel and do things differently. I have a
> new beginning. Thank you for that.

A community member reflected on the fears she had before going
into the Circle:

> I was really worried about what would explode in the
> Circle. Man, there were a lot of angry people coming.
> We even thought of putting the Circle off. Well, it did
> explode; we were right about that. But we were wrong
> about the damage that anger exploding in a Circle would
> cause. It brought a lot of things out, and people worked
> through it. They really did well. The best thing we did
> was not to cancel the Circle. It's the same thing we need
> to learn every time: Trust the Circle.

A defense counsel described how having community members who were ex-offenders affected new applicants:

> I think the very best thing that happened in the beginning of the Circle was for Jessie [the offender] to see and hear Jim [a previous offender in the Circle] speak for himself. It made Jessie realize that if Jim could do this, so could he, and seeing how much support Jim got from his Circle moved Jessie's attitude and hope a long way.

Justice professionals benefit from participating in the Circle as well. Judge Gary Schurrer reflects on how the Circle affected him:

> The Circle is healing for justice officials as well. It brings people together. It improves that human-being-to-human-being contact.

Comments from the offenders themselves often include surprise about how hard Circles can be, yet how profound their personal change has been as a result. The following reflections are not uncommon:

> I thought it would be easier. I didn't want to go to jail. I thought the Circle would give me an easier sentence. It was anything but easier, but it got me to where I am today, and jail wouldn't have done that. What is scary is that if I'd known—really known—how tough it was going to be in Circle, I'd have gone to court and gone to jail, and this is the scary part, where would I be now?

> If it weren't for the Circle and all the caring and support and the wisdom of the Circle, I'd be dead.

STAGE 4. FOLLOW-UP: MAKING IT WORK— ACCOUNTABILITY AND IMPLEMENTING CIRCLE CONSENSUS

A successful Circle gathering by no means ends the process but rather gives everyone a fresh start—a new foundation from which to work on the issues. The challenge in stage 4 is for everyone to translate the promises of the consensus agreement into reality. Follow-up is critical, for without it, hopes and plans go unrealized, and old patterns reemerge. People lose faith in the Circle process, in the agreements made, and in each other. Everyone needs to know that what happened in the Circle was more than just talk.

When beginning to use Circles, communities may overlook the importance of follow-up. In time, they recognize its importance. At Roca:

> Follow-up is now recognized as one of the greatest challenges of the successful use of Circles: if an agreement is made in the Circle, it is important that someone follow up to see if people are accountable to those agreements. If strong emotions are shared, there needs to be follow-up with individuals to see how they are doing and ensure that they are getting the support they need.[24]

The follow-up process continually seeks ways for Circles to strengthen the positive, healing connections within communities, to extend a community's capacity to be self-reliant, and to share responsibility for dealing with crime and thus preventing future harms. Follow-up sustains the momentum of Circles. Some basic measures help communities do this—i.e., strengthen everyone's accountability to the Circle process and to each other, especially in criminal justice cases.

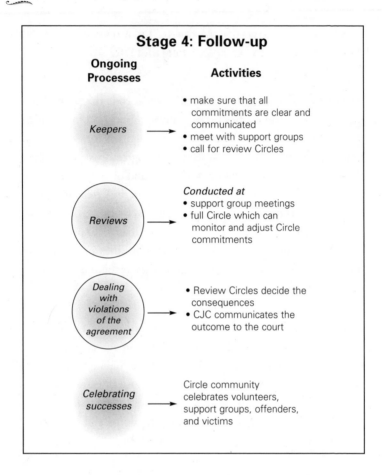

Stage 4: Follow-up

Ongoing Processes	Activities
Keepers	• make sure that all commitments are clear and communicated • meet with support groups • call for review Circles
Reviews	*Conducted at* • support group meetings • full Circle which can monitor and adjust Circle commitments
Dealing with violations of the agreement	• Review Circles decide the consequences • CJC communicates the outcome to the court
Celebrating successes	Circle community celebrates volunteers, support groups, offenders, and victims

Holding regular reviews

When offenders, support groups, and agency professionals know a review Circle will evaluate what they have or haven't done to honor their Circle commitments, they're more motivated to act. But it isn't only the review per se that makes this measure so effective. Regular Circles create a different quality of commitment. Being accountable to oneself and to one's entire community carries much greater weight as an incentive to "get it done" than merely reporting to a paid probation officer or facing up to a busy judge. For most offenders and others in the Circle, their image and reputation are at stake not with strangers but with those who have known them all their lives. They've made commitments to people who either have been or will be personally involved with helping them make positive changes.

By the time offenders reach the review Circle, most are sufficiently comfortable with the Circle process to speak on their own behalf. Many take enormous pride in speaking for themselves about both their efforts and their successes. An offender who had spent almost half his adult life in jail actually looked forward to his review Circle:

> No one ever could have convinced me that one day I'd
> look forward to going to court. Well, Circles are really
> not like court, I know that, but you know what I mean.
> I look forward to my reviews in the Circles, because I
> want to prove to them that I'm doing well. Doing good
> gives me back my pride and makes them see that they can
> trust me. That's a really big thing for me, really big.

Review Circles fine-tune everyone's obligations. However promising plans may be, when reality hits, the offender or the community may realize they've bitten off more than they can chew. Reviews deal with unexpected changes and make needed adjustments. By working with people through everyday challenges, review Circles ensure either that the job gets done or that the consensus is altered in ways everyone can understand, accept, and manage.

For example, Circle members working with a young man named Henry became frustrated when several months went by, and he still hadn't taken the anger management classes included in his social compact with the Circle. Each time he had an excuse, yet he seemed to be dragging his feet. When they pressed him on the matter at a review Circle, Henry exploded, "I've done those anger management classes before! They're no good! There's something wrong with my head. What I need is a psychiatrist." As the talking piece went around the Circle, members acknowledged Henry's courage to speak his truth, which he clearly had not felt safe to express at the time the social compact was developed. Together they decided to change his social compact by replacing his anger management class with one-on-one sessions with a psychologist. By the next Circle, Henry had begun those sessions, and he never missed one.

Whether it's helping offenders break addictions; find and hold jobs; arrange housing and transportation; obtain proper treatment, counseling, or medical care; finish their education; or sort through personal, legal, or financial issues, participants who promised support need to deliver on their commitments. When they can't, others need to be found who can, or the agreed-upon level of support needs to be adjusted. Doing nothing isn't an option, for that leads to all kinds of negative assumptions and undermines the relationships and positive expectations born in the Circle. If the Circle community and support groups don't follow through, offenders feel betrayed. Other offenders may hesitate to choose Circles if they believe the community isn't dependable.

Review Circles boost people's resolve by reminding them of the Circle's vision and of their pledge of time and energy. When unanticipated circumstances arise, review Circles adjust the promises, so that, instead of collapsing, the Circle's consensus is renewed. They clarify who's doing what and how it's going, as well as develop realistic deadlines for completing objectives. They identify both the strengths and the weaknesses in the original consensus agreement. And they readily detect when something isn't working—when the plan needs to be fine-tuned or changed. At each step, review Circles both catch backsliding and celebrate progress.

Most important, review Circles sustain the communal spirit

initiated in the Circle—the feeling of taking responsibility, working together, and making a difference. A volunteer vividly expressed the sense of being an instrumental part of a community:

> After the first Circle, I went home exhausted. Damn,
> that was hard work. I was excited by what happened, but
> drained. I didn't think I'd be back—too difficult. That
> was years ago, it seems. I've come to all of the Circles,
> because this is the place I deeply feel I'm a part of my
> community. And it's the place I feel we are making a
> difference—where a difference must be made. We are
> not just changing lives; we are making a community by
> working through our differences.

In review Circles, participants are accountable to one another, which means they act on their responsibilities and commitments. These can change, and there can be multiple ways to meet them, but changes must be worked out through the Circle process. Following through on commitments to the Circle builds confidence in the process, whereas failing to do so undermines trust in it. Because the Circle's effectiveness can be at stake, especially in criminal justice cases, everyone is responsible for monitoring how agreements are being kept on all sides and for sharing accountability for the Circle process.

Maintaining good communication with the larger community

Wherever possible, to attract broad-based support, keepers regularly inform the larger community about how the consensus is being carried out. Unfounded rumors about a violation can be as damaging to community trust as an actual violation. Community support depends upon knowing both the success stories and what is done if something goes wrong.

Sharing responsibility

Consensus follow-up should be carried out in teams. Not only does this reflect the Circle vision of building relationships and communities as the larger solution to crime, but it's also practical. Responsibilities should be shared, so that a few people aren't left shouldering the workload. Then, when a volunteer must nurse a sick family member or go to a child's soccer game, the person doesn't feel torn about whether to honor the Circle commitment or to take care of his or her own family and needs. Another volunteer on the team can step in and carry out a Circle commitment.

Moreover, having a few do everything isn't sustainable. It fails to build a sense of shared responsibility and places too much emphasis on a "super-volunteer." The idea of Circles isn't to replace community dependence on a few professionals with dependence on a few "super-volunteers." It's to engage a broad cross-section in community building—a lot of people doing a little, rather than a few people doing a lot.

If the community becomes dependent on a few super-volunteers and they burn out, what then? Professionals end up stepping in—those who are paid to monitor behavior—and the energy shifts from the cooperative atmosphere of the Circle to the coercive authority of the system.

When volunteers from the community stay involved beyond sentencing, the rate of Circle successes substantially increases. Volunteers make important contributions to support groups and review Circles, because they widen the perspective and lend a larger sense of what's being accomplished. Offenders are inspired and motivated when virtual strangers volunteer their time, skills, knowledge, and efforts to helping them turn their lives around. Speaking of a volunteer on his support team, Michael said:

It was three in the morning. I couldn't go another minute without a drink. I had to drink—or call Gary. I called Gary. He was there, like right away. We talked till dawn, had some breakfast, and I made it. I would never have called my probation officer, and even if I did, it wouldn't have been the same thing. Gary came. No one was paying him to come. He came because he cared enough for me to make it. Things like that came all the time from my support group. That's why I made it.

Recognizing success

Celebrating the progress of victims in surviving, offenders in changing, and community volunteers in supporting helps everyone stay motivated. Both small steps and larger milestones warrant recognition. Sometimes communities hold a dinner to honor contributions and progress. Displaying a wall of photographs of support groups for victims and offenders can serve to remind people of what has been done and give a sense of history. The work of healing from trauma and changing lives is intense, including as it does periods of frustration and despair. Recognizing successes gives people strength and perspective during the darker times that every Circle faces.

What counts as success? It may be that the offender's violations are less frequent and less serious, or that his or her substance abuse decreases. Or it may be that the community joins together to respond to challenges. Certainly for victims, success involves some repair of the harm done to them. Success also means that victims receive full and ongoing support on their journeys. Communities must carefully consider how they measure success, because that often determines where they focus and what improves through the work they do.

Rethinking failure: accountability to the Circle

Recognizing that despairing times are an inevitable part of change, we need to consider what counts as a failure in Circle work. It's not when an applicant fails to stick to agreements. Profound life shifts usually involve moving forward and stepping back many times before a new way settles in. Failure would be for a Circle to do nothing about the applicant's relapses, or worse, to give up on the Circle process altogether. People join Circles, not because life is easy, but because life is painfully hard sometimes, and because people in crisis need help from supportive relationships to pull through and move in positive directions. The following comments came from a community discussion about an applicant who relapsed into substance abuse after a year of staying clean of drugs and crime:

- "At worst, Benny failed, but we did not. We learned a lot from each other, and we are still working together."
- "We trust, understand, and respect each other much more now than before. We can thank him for giving us the opportunity to achieve all that."
- "All of us feel more a part of our community than ever before."
- "If Benny repeats, it means we try again. We can't really afford to give up."
- "Offenders like Benny have a long history of abuse, low self-esteem, and disempowerment. It will take time for him to be empowered and healed."
- "There are no miracle cures, but we did find people in communities with miraculous patience and caring."
- "Doctors do not give up if the first treatment fails. Why should the community?"

When offenders keep their commitments to the Circle and their community, they earn redemption. Dennis Maloney, who pioneered community and restorative justice practices in Deschutes County, Oregon, believes that when offenders meet their commitments, "the community has a responsibility to take the scarlet letter off their forehead and celebrate that they've earned the grace of redemption and their respected place in the community."

Whereas the Circle gathering explores the potential for individuals and the community to be together in new ways, follow-up makes that potential a reality. It puts the new ways into practice, creating patterns that step-by-step lead to a new culture. Follow-up helps everyone transfer what they've learned in the sacred space of Circle to the ordinary space of daily life.

With every step of follow-up, the principles underlying Circles should continue to guide our interactions. Trust, courage, inclusivity, sharing, understanding, forgiveness, humility, respect, equality, love: these and all the other values still apply. Yet these values may be unwittingly undermined whenever offenders are treated as lesser beings assumed to be irresponsible until proven otherwise, or whenever victims are treated in condescending ways or told what they should do, such as forgive, heal, "get over it," or "find closure and move on."

How individuals work through the processes of life is sacred, involving a unique path that has its own timing. The course someone follows isn't for another to judge. Each person's choice of path warrants respect, since that's how we honor each other's autonomy. Indeed, holding offenders accountable for their actions toward others, especially toward those they've harmed, respects them as equals and forms a basis for more healthy future relationships.

Honoring collective autonomy is important for communities as well. As they share responsibility for dealing with crime and preventing future harm, communities gain pride and respect in their power to set their own course. They also lay the ground-work for healthier relationships among all the individuals, groups, and sectors within them. Using Circles to respond to hurts and conflicts, communities prove their self-reliance and gain trust in their own capacities, where before despair prevailed. One keeper observed:

> Ultimately, I know it's worth it. I know it's worth it when I see John [an ex-offender] out there in our community walking with his kids, being with his family. I know I was—that we all were—part of making that happen. I know, too, that we may not see success happen like that right away—that it will take patience when the person we're helping goes through many bad times. But I believe we're planting seeds in that person. They know we're here to help, and that gives them what they often need to make that turn in their life. Our being here makes a big difference. When they're ready to turn, I hope we'll still be here, ready to help.

Chapter Six

Stepping Back to Count Circle Gains

> *There are many persons ready to do what is right, because in their hearts they know what is right. But they hesitate, waiting for the other fellow to make the first move—and he, in turn, waits for you. The minute a person whose word means a great deal dares to take the openhearted and courageous way, many others will follow.*
>
> —MARIAN ANDERSON
> African American contralto, 1956

BRINGING CIRCLES INTO A COMMUNITY generates benefits far beyond the immediate needs of addressing crime. Whereas the crime-focused outcomes are "curative"—mending or healing a specific harm—other benefits are "preventive," rendering crime no longer the overriding issue. Expressed positively, Circles are about building healthy communities. Not only do they use crises to address unseen or untreated ills, but they also use the peace-making process to strengthen people, families, and relationships. Yet even this isn't the sum of the gains they offer.

By training people over time to respond to hurts and conflicts differently, Circles serve as midwives to the paradigm shift described in chapter 1. They offer a public forum where people can develop the physical, mental, emotional, and spiritual habits of peacemaking. Few other forums exist for doing this.

For participants, the training in this paradigm shift happens almost imperceptibly from the ongoing personal experience of being in Circle. The shift isn't abstract but grounded. It affects not only the intellectual, emotional, or spiritual sides of us but all of

them together in a physically present process. And the shift occurs
not only in theory but also in solid, often demanding practice.

Moreover, the training in peacemaking begins with those present but ripples out. Certainly the victims and offenders as well as
their families and friends experience something new—a process
that listens to them and takes their needs seriously as a condition
for positive change. Community members also have an opportunity to be involved in creating substantive change—a paradigm
shift from the alienation and passivity that can become the norm.
People from the justice system are exposed to the paradigm shift
too, some directly, others by word of mouth. And all the wider sectors that Circles call upon as resources and that may turn to Circles
for help—schools, faith groups, businesses, social services—witness
a paradigm shift in how to be a community by resolving conflicts in
open, respectful, and mutually supportive ways.

In a nutshell, Circles generate long-term personal, relational,
community, system, and cultural transformation. Evidence for this
transformation is found in a community's increased capacity to resolve differences and to forge outside-the-box solutions. But Circles
generate less tangible fruits as well—understanding, trust, empathy,
love, as well as a greater awareness of how connected we are. The
more Circles yield these intangible results, the easier it is for people
to achieve the more tangible outcomes—agreements, plans for
implementation, or joint projects. Circles are not, therefore, about
dispensing quick fixes but about crafting deep, sustainable changes.
Based on our experiences and those of others, here are some of these
wider gains.

The Circle process builds relationships

From repairing broken bonds to creating new ones, building relationships is by far the most important outcome of Circles.
Reaching consensus and finding innovative solutions are valuable

results, but they're not as valuable to peacemaking as nurturing a deeper sense of connectedness. Strengthening our relationships provides the foundation for all the other outcomes of Circles.

When we started using Circles, the implications of this didn't hit us. We didn't realize that Circles' primary contribution to sentencing would be building bonds not only within communities but also between communities and state agencies. These bonds expand the resources for responding to needs, but they also dramatically change how everyone looks at the problems that cause crime. In Circles, responsibility for crime is seen as belonging not solely to any one person or agency but to the larger community. Participants share responsibility both for what went wrong and for working to correct it. The more experience people have in Circles, the more they appreciate what this can mean. In their Circle work, the young people at Roca speak about discovering the power of "we." Carolyn Boyes-Watson explains:

> The Circle process is about recognizing the power we hold collectively. By creating a space where all voices can be heard equally and where people can recognize their shared values and common interests across social differences, the Circle opens an opportunity for a sense of "we" that seeks solutions rather than demands that others fix or correct problems. Sister Josefa talks about the power of the Circle to help people to know what they are capable of; Sayra talks about the shift among young people from asking staff to respond to negative behavior to taking responsibility themselves for holding one another accountable; and Saroeum talks of the willingness of people to change: the power of the Circle lies within the people in the Circle.[25]

This trust in collective power grows as people share their values and pursue common hopes for what a community can be.

Michael Glennon, a victim-services advocate for Suffolk County, Massachusetts, comments on his experience in Circles:

> The beauty of this is that people are coming together trying to find common purpose, believing in the same things, building trust and relationships. People don't get to spend time together in common purpose.[26]

The Circle process breaks through isolation

As people feel more related, they feel less isolated. This is an obvious but important deduction, since feeling alone—separate and detached from others—can intensify a crisis. Few people thrive in isolation, yet that's exactly how we feel in the middle of trauma or upheaval. Experiencing ourselves as isolated makes a hard situation worse, because it cuts us off from the resources we have, both in ourselves and in families and communities, to turn things around. We make narrow assumptions about what's possible, and we begin to believe no one can help us through the crisis. One offender, after spending a year in the Circle process, expressed what a difference it made for him to break through years of feeling isolated:

> I'd always been alone, you know, since I started getting into trouble at thirteen. My family kinda gave up on me. Part of the anger in me came from feeling alone. All them professionals—my P.O. [probation officer] and social worker—they kept changing. It was a job to them. They were part of the system, not family to me. I didn't ever trust any of 'em. So at first I really didn't trust the people who connected up with me in the Circle. Now that I've seen how they stay with me, I do trust 'em. And not feeling alone has made the difference for me.

Isolation clearly hinders the healing process for victims and offenders, but it also prevents those of us who are professionals in the system from fully experiencing the depth of transformation that Circles offer. Acting from narrowly defined roles, locked behind the institutionalized barriers that reinforce our isolation, we lose our connection both to our inner values and to the communities we serve. Terry Reardon, the Chief of Police of the Revere Police Department in Massachusetts, described how different Circles can be for justice professionals in experiencing not only victims and offenders but also each other:

> You meet people [in Circle] and they talk from their
> heart, and you see that they are not whatever your pre-
> conceptions of them were before you were in the room.
> Not only that . . . but there were other people from vari-
> ous parts of the criminal justice system—juvenile proba-
> tion, juvenile corrections—and you see that people are
> people. They may have these jobs and work for these
> monolithic institutions, but nevertheless, when it comes
> down to it, they are still people, so for that fact, you make
> a lot of friends, instead of thinking about how you can
> make an end run around this one. . . . It absolutely opens
> up lines of communication previously non-existent . . .
> and you are able to connect with people other than on a
> professional basis. . . . They see you for who you are . . .
> a human being. . . . You are not just a cop or just a
> social worker. . . . It brings it down to a much more
> personal level.[27]

In Circles, a professional connects as a person first. Interacting on a first-name basis helps remove the isolating barriers of position, allowing the community to see the person behind the professional role. Vichey Phoung observed:

> In a Circle, you don't come as anybody else but your-
> self. . . . For example . . . police officers, or mayors in
> the community don't get to come as police or mayors
> really but just as concerned citizens—really to voice their
> opinions as that. . . .'Cause all the time we come to meet,
> we're separated from one another by titles. . . . We come
> as this or that. . . . But in Circle, I don't care if you are
> this or that, you sort of leave that outside the door and
> really bring yourself, and it's really about bonding and
> getting to know each other.[28]

His brother, Saroeum Phoung, agreed:

> You could be the judge, but you gotta come as a human. . . .
> You could be non-educated, but you'd be alright, 'cause
> people will respect your feelings. So no matter what age,
> ethnicity, gender, or whatever, you get to come to the
> Circle as a human, and there's always a place for you.[29]

From the opening to the closing rituals, Circles affirm how connected we are. They call upon our bonds with others—families, friends, neighbors, coworkers—to help us work through adverse circumstances and traumas.

Circles attend to less obvious, more challenging connections as well, opening dialogues between those who are deeply divided within a community. Being in Circle with the "enemy" is powerful. At Roca, for example, Circles have brought together youth and police. In the course of dialogue, the youth see police as humans and in turn feel they're being seen as human beings and listened to as well.[30] For those who spent years fighting the police and feeling great hostility around them, the experience can be transforming.

The Circle process fosters open dialogue

Coming together as fellow human beings—beyond roles and animosities—enables participants to work through issues *with* others rather than *against* them. In Circles, people often release differences and hurts in order to seek solutions that embrace everyone's interests. Through open dialogue, people join in a quest to understand a situation's complexity and the human needs involved. In this context, expressing differences doesn't lead to further opposition but to a better grasp of what's at stake. Sometimes interjecting apparently unrelated comments—stories, needs, experiences, or feelings—can trigger breakthroughs. They may inspire others to share of themselves too, or they may lend new perspectives that suggest unconventional solutions. In Circles, open exploration becomes contagious, training people in an essential skill of peacemaking.

The Circle process encourages value-based actions

At the opening of the book, we posed this question: How can we live together without harming each other? To phrase it differently, what can serve as a reliable touchstone for conduct, so our actions contribute to making a good life together? Much of our culture responds to this question with the model of rewards and punishments—that external incentives keep us in line. In court, for example, the threat of greater punishment or the reward of a reduced sentence are the primary tools used to change destructive behavior.

Rewards and punishments may have their uses in extreme situations for short-term effects, but they rarely inspire the transformation that generates lasting changes. The reason is simple: reward-punishment mechanisms control behavior by replacing internal with external motivation. That is, they emphasize the external incentives of chasing carrots or avoiding sticks rather than call upon personal values to generate responsible conduct. When rewards and punishments are no longer present, people often revert to former habits. As one ex-offender said, "I played along until my probation order was over."

Circles promote a shift from the external back to the internal. When core values drive the desire to change, these values sustain us past temptations—past the shelf life of any external reward or punishment. Instead of being externally driven, we learn to act according to our deepest values—respect, trust, honesty, and all the other values that provide the inner frame of Circles. An ex-offender and Circle participant observed:

> I know how to play the game. I know what to do and
> say in court, how to get past my P.O. [probation officer].
> It was all like a con game. You got rewarded if you were
> good at it, shot down if you weren't. I couldn't play the
> game in the Circle, first, because everyone there knew
> me. But most of all, somehow it didn't fit. The deeper
> the Circle dug into me, the more of me came out.
>
>   I had been doing things because of my needs—what I
> thought was important for me—but what I thought was
> important really changed [in the Circle].

Because rewards and punishments focus on externals, using them to manage behavior fails to fix the deeper problems, which are internal. If we feel disconnected from our inner lives, imposing external controls further disconnects us. More specifically, if our inner lives are filled with pain, which our behavior then passes on to others, imposing external controls doesn't heal the pain and can make it worse. Instead of helping us clarify our core values and act from them, an externally controlling approach attempts to coerce us.

Yet most people resist coercion, even by rewards.[31] Those who can't escape external controls often resist by simply "playing the game," "playing the system." Of the many juvenile programs and facilities she had been sent to, Priscilla said, "They were all pretty much the same. Talking down. . . . But I said to myself that I wasn't going to change until I wanted to change."[32]

For Priscilla, Circles were her turning point. In them, people listened to what was within her—her pain and anger from years of victimization. Circles gave her a chance to reconnect with her inner truth and to have it received by others. Circle members heard her with empathy and accepted her feelings. The experience changed her.

Like Priscilla, we tend to change only when we want to—when we're inwardly moved to do so. Circles can reawaken this inner direction. By definition, inner direction cannot be imposed from without, though it can be supported. A space can be held where inner motivation can grow, and this is what Circles aspire to do. To invite inwardly born levels of change, Circles shift the focus from outer to inner experiences. As we each reconnect with what's within, positive changes come from our own yearnings to live meaningfully, based on our values.

Naturally, restraining hurtful behavior is essential. Circles respond by discussing the values participants need to honor and to have honored in order to work through their pain, conflicts, and differences in a good way. Inner rather than outer factors restrain harmful conduct—not just to escape punishment or capture a reward, but to be someone quite different, someone whose values inform behavior.

To help offenders make the shift, Circles may use external restraints as short-term control mechanisms while they help offenders develop their own healthy internal controls. If offenders don't respond to an inner, value-based approach, more external means of restraint are necessary, and the court will often be a more suitable process than a Circle for these individuals.

Who is or isn't ready to make the shift becomes clear during the Circle process. It can't be known beforehand. Circle dialogue creates a space for self-discovery—for going places rarely visited and exploring values not otherwise perceived as useful to survival. A judge and Circle participant for more than two decades, Barry has had a hard time assessing who might respond to the Circle's call to inner values and who might have become too dependent on external restraints:

> Alive as I am to the profound potential of a Circle to change behavior, as a judge, I have felt that people who've spent many years within institutions—and who seem completely absorbed in the "con game" that they've needed to survive inside those institutions—were never going to connect to the deeper place of inner values through the Circle process. I believed that a reward-punishment model, being all they ever knew, would be all that could ever contain their antisocial behavior.
>
> Recently, I was wrong again. Charlie was before the Circle for a break-and-enter into a home, committed within weeks of his release from prison. This was exactly the same offense that had sent him to jail for sentences ranging from two to five years many, many times before. The victims, who had confronted and struggled with Charlie in their home, participated in his Circle. I'd like to think I was not alone in wondering why the community would invest their energies in someone like Charlie.
>
> At the beginning, Charlie looked and talked as if the Circle were just a new con game. It is now almost three years since Charlie's first Circle. It has been a long road for Charlie, for me, and for many others in his Circles. He relapsed twice into substance abuse. Both times he eagerly sought help. He has not committed any new of-

fenses. Charlie had never previously gone a year—and sometimes not even a month—out of jail without committing an offense.

I was unable to recognize Charlie's potential to change, even after the first Circle. He did discover his inner truth and values, and for three years, he has steadfastly followed the road these values call him to walk.

For twenty-five years, the reward-punishment model had not changed his antisocial behavior. If anything, that model of behavioral change had driven him deeper into antisocial behavior and further from his inner values. In the Circle, Charlie's journey of self-discovery and connecting to inner values gave him a new perspective on what his life could be. He said, "I feel more like myself. I always wanted to connect in a good way with people, not to use them for what I could get. Now I give to others and help them. That feels good to me."

Charlie's example of working hard to align his life with his core values has become an invaluable asset to many. He is a sign of hope, a sign that we can never fail to try. In his last Circle, all of us—the victims, the justice professionals, community leaders, and volunteers—expressed our appreciation to Charlie for inspiring us to believe in ourselves, in others, and in the power of connecting.

I shiver to think of the many, many times I have wielded the threat of a harsh punishment and held out the carrot of a lesser punishment, hoping to change behavior. How many of these times did I inadvertently push people away from aligning their lives with their values?

Circles encourage participants to align their conduct with their values not just in Circle but in every area of life. By making Circles a common feature in all aspects of their work, the Roca community has come to view them not as a program but as a way to be. Carolyn Boyes-Watson explains:

> The Circle is a commitment to practice living the values of the Circle. The more people sit in Circle at Roca, the more they have learned that Circle is not about sitting in the physical space but about how to be in Circle when you are not in Circle. The meaning of "being in Circle" has expanded to refer to acting in a "Circle way" or holding oneself "in a good way" in one's relationship with others and oneself.[33]

She goes on to discuss how bringing Circle values into a community or organization to this extent inevitably shifts the culture of the group, as it has at Roca:

> There is . . . the understanding that this is not a process that is done once and for all, but a way of life: constantly working to "be in a good way" with oneself and with others. This lesson, more than any other, has led to a profound shift within the organizational culture at Roca. . . . Among the staff, there is a sense that conversations are more respectful, more joyful and more appreciative of each other. For everyone concerned, the reason is that there is a conscious awareness of being in Circle when they are not in Circle. Accountability to the values of the Circles extends far beyond the physical space of the Circle process.[34]

The Circle process provides a place to acknowledge responsibility

Acting on values calls us to take responsibility for our actions, especially since failing to do so blocks healing and erodes relationships. In Circles, accepting responsibility isn't about shaming, blaming, or placing guilt. Circles treat everyone as having value no matter what they may have done. Because Circles hold everyone equally in a respectful way, each person's dignity and worth are not in question. People feel safe enough to acknowledge responsibility for their conduct, trusting that others won't use it against them or think less of them as human beings.

In this constructive context, acknowledging responsibility fosters respect and improves relationships—not only for offenders but for the larger community as well. For example, acknowledging how we ourselves might have contributed to the breakdown of a relationship makes it easier for others to do the same. Peacemaking Circles invite such shared reflections. Participants explore how they might have added to a misunderstanding or even given energies to an underlying cause of a crime. The goal isn't to point fingers but to find areas of unclaimed power. Being holistic in approach, Circles generate a larger perspective, and this holistic view makes it easier for people to see their piece of responsibility. The intent is persistently constructive: understanding how everyone shares some responsibility provides clues for how people can work together to turn things around.

The Circle process facilitates innovative problem-solving

When we're alone and isolated, our view is limited. Instead of seeing many options, we think we have few, if any. Again, relationships put us on a different track. By bringing together diverse perspectives, Circles foster creative problem-solving. They generate alternatives that those in crisis either couldn't previously imagine or assumed were impossible. In most sentencing Circles, no one could have predicted the outcome. By harnessing the collective imagination, Circles take novel approaches to sentencing, addressing needs and harms in ways law books simply couldn't prescribe. These innovative sentences often bridge differences and bring together what seemed like hopelessly polarized positions. Drawing out this kind of energy and imagination requires a safe place, which is why Circles are able to produce such creative, individualized results.

The Circle process brings healing and transformation

Healing is essential to the Circle process, both as a means of change and as an outcome. Though Circles don't make healing happen, the Circle process is conducive to healing. As people experience their collective powers of creative problem-solving, for example, their sense of life's possibilities shifts. They begin to heal from being stuck in closed-loop, self-destructive patterns. Or, as people share their pain, act from their values, build relationships, and acknowledge responsibility, they begin to heal from damaged self-esteem.

Indeed, crime calls for healing in every direction, since wounds are not only an outcome of crime but often its cause. Crime is all tangled up in woundedness. In some communities, a victim in one case is an offender in another. Hurtful conduct often comes from those who carry a heavy burden of unresolved fear, shame, pain, and pent-up anger at being abused or neglected. Yet in acting out their hurt on others, offenders further wound themselves, since harming another violates one's soul. By acknowledging both the immediate and the underlying wounds of crime, Circles are often able to break the cycle of woundedness.

Circles address wounds in various ways. Based on the Medicine Wheel teaching of balance, Circle philosophy regards the wounds of crime as physical, mental, emotional, and spiritual in nature and hence as needing attention on all these dimensions. As wounds are uncovered and cleansed on each level, they begin to heal. The various features of Circles—e.g., the storytelling, the practice of equality, the relationship building, the sense of empowerment, and the atmosphere of care and empathy—all promote healing, largely because they make honest expressions of feelings and vulnerability less threatening. "We meet at our woundedness," stated a participant at a Circle training. Connections made in a space of vulnerability and of needing one another in a healing process form deep bonds, and they can support profound change.

As healing unfolds, the negative energies around wounds—the energies of anger, fear, shame, resentment, and self-protection—can be released and replaced by the positive energies flowing from connection, hope, compassion for ourselves and others, and a shared vision. Circles change the way our energies flow in relationships. We slow down and listen to each other, and this opens the door to deep change. Don Johnson reflects on why this happens so consistently:

> One reason that Circles work is that most of the time we spend in them is spent in silence. We create a pause where someone can be heard with a loving ear. I think we often run on habit energy. Pausing or stopping in order to listen gives us a chance to change our patterns. The personal silence we experience in Circles offers us one of those moments when transformation can take place.

People often emerge from Circles feeling differently about themselves. They discover capacities for interacting with others—both in how they're treated and in how they respond—that they may never have experienced before. James Roche, a staff member of Roca, noted such healing changes in himself:

> I look at myself two or three years ago, and I'm handling myself better, and that's because of Circle. . . . And I know it's okay now to live, 'cause life can be positive and be

okay, and [you can] be allowed to make mistakes and forgive and forgive yourself. . . . At the end of the day, to know that the only person you can change is yourself—I think Circles have helped me understand that.[35]

These transformative processes are not reserved, though, for those in crisis. Because the wounds of crime extend in many directions—to victims, their families and friends, to community members, and to the families and friends of offenders—Circles create a space to support the healing journeys of everyone involved. Our experience, consistent with the wisdom of many indigenous cultures, suggests that the suffering of anyone affects everyone. Suffering causes an imbalance within any community, leaving everyone in need of healing. Indeed, the community or society as a whole most likely contains hurtful patterns which the suffering brought to light. When Circles embark on healing the specific wounds surrounding a crime, they are actually engaged in community healing.

The Circle process addresses the deeper causes of conflict

As people feel more connected in Circles, tensions begin to resolve in unexpected ways. Participants realize that the crime was a symptom of deeper issues. Understanding this and pulling together to do something about it, participants begin to tackle the larger issues—social, economic, educational, political, racial, philosophical, institutional, governmental, or religious—that cause disharmony and that can culminate in crime. The more Circles address these deeper causes of crime, the more effective their long-term outcomes.

The result is that people reclaim their communities. Close to home, they take stock of human needs and explore how the community can rally to meet them. But they also look at what's behind community ills and seek ways to address the deeper causes of imbalance. Circles are a gentle, peaceful, yet persistent and powerful force for social change, because they instill in participants the conviction that communities are what we make them and that our power and options for shaping them are vastly greater than we imagined—if we practice coming together in a good way.

The Circle process generates a systemic view

In our age of ecology, we've learned to think in systems—whole systems whose patterns extend far beyond what's immediately visible. In his book *The Fifth Discipline*, business consultant and systems thinker Peter Senge explains the necessity of taking a systemic view if we're seeking fundamental solutions to our problems:

> A cloud masses, the sky darkens, leaves twist upward, and we know that it will rain. We also know that after the storm, the runoff will feed into groundwater miles away, and the sky will grow clear by tomorrow. All these events are distant in time and space, and yet they are all connected within the same pattern. Each has an influence on the rest, an influence that is usually hidden from view. You can only understand the system of a rainstorm by contemplating the whole, not any individual part of the pattern. Business and other human endeavors are also systems. They, too, are bound by invisible fabrics of interrelated actions, which often take years to fully play out their effects on each other. Since we are part of that lacework ourselves, it's doubly hard to see the whole pattern of change. Instead, we tend to focus on snapshots of isolated parts of the system, and wonder why our deepest problems never seem to get solved.[36]

To resolve crimes in ways that respect all interests and address deeper causes, we need the whole picture, yet no one person has this. By bringing together all those affected by a crime, Circles provide the means for remedying this. All perspectives are given voice and respected, which expands everyone's grasp of how the crime has affected each person. Exploring the past, present, and future, participants learn the histories of each person leading up to the event, the full implications of the crime in the present, and how the crime impacts each person's sense of the future. They ponder the rainstorm's total pattern, seen and unseen.

To further broaden the view, Circles draw in not only those immediately affected, including justice system personnel, but also people from different walks of life, including faith communities, schools, businesses, and related social agencies. The wider the range of perspectives represented in a Circle, the greater the sense of shared responsibility, the broader the vision of what happened and what can be done, the greater the resources for making change, and, hence, the more encompassing the outcome.

Such a systemic view challenges us to consider how we ourselves might be contributing to breakdowns, so we can figure out how to work together to prevent them and better serve our common objectives. The recent case of *R. v. Jacob* (Territorial Court of Yukon, 2002) illustrates the tragedies that can follow when many well-meaning, well-trained people fail to collaborate. A young man named Marcel Jacob pled guilty to a vicious rape of a stranger. His history under state care revealed that everyone—social workers, foster parents, family members, school teachers, psychologists, lawyers, judges, and community members—did their jobs individually, yet all failed to change his obviously inappropriate sexual behavior, which led to a vicious crime. Many made valiant individual efforts to help him; many burned out and gave up; and many knew something terrible would happen. Nothing deterred Marcel Jacob from his tragic rendezvous, principally because the system wasn't set up for collaborating on the overall handling of his case. Yet without this professional and community collaboration, his case couldn't be treated in a systemic way, and the underlying causes of his crime couldn't be addressed.

In so many cases of young people obviously headed for serious crime, each of the many professionals who intervene in their lives may do *their job*, but *the job*—namely, effective intervention—is not done. For that, the families, communities, and professionals need a systemic approach, which no one can achieve alone. Circles respond directly to this need. They rally the energy, skills, and resources to effectively intervene in a situation that seems mired in destructive patterns. First they generate a collective awareness of the larger job to be done, and then they start mobilizing the means to do it.

Ultimately, nothing less than this systemic view can respond to crime in the healing ways—curative and preventive—that we as a society seek. During a sensational murder trial in the late 1920s, famed lawyer Clarence Darrow argued for a systemic, holistic approach:

> I know, Your Honor, that every atom of life in all this
> universe is bound up together. I know that a pebble can-
> not be thrown into the ocean without disturbing every
> drop of water in the sea. I know that every life is inex-
> tricably mixed and woven with every other life. I know
> that every influence, conscious and unconscious, acts and
> reacts on every living organism, and that no one can fix
> the blame.[37]

In other words, crime isn't a superficial blot on the landscape; it's a systemic reality. Crime brings hidden ills into focus, dramatizing them in ways we can no longer ignore. "If we look at who is in prison," one justice professional observed, "we can see what the social ills are."

Changing the patterns that lead to crime and that follow from it cannot be done piecemeal. With our best intentions and considerable resources, we have tried. A systemic view calls us to change our strategy—to join forces and use the full capacity of our communities to respond to crime in all its dimensions. Circles offer the means to do this—to take a systemic approach.

The Circle process empowers participants and communities

The net effect of all these Circle outcomes is that participants feel empowered in life-changing ways. They learn that they can take charge of their lives and turn them in new directions, confident that they'll get the support they need to do this. Victims, offenders, justice professionals, and community members find they're able to resolve problems far more constructively than they ever thought possible.

Specifically, in the aftermath of crime, victims may feel powerless and without control over their interests, alone and isolated. By respecting their voice and needs, Circles create a space for them to regain their autonomy. If victims choose not to participate in a Circle involving the offender, they still feel respected by knowing they have the right to do so. Whatever their choice, the Circle process empowers victims to reengage with their personal and public communities and to obtain whatever help they need as they do this.

Offenders also feel empowered both by having a voice in the peacemaking process and by being held accountable for their actions. Circles treat offenders as if they're capable of being responsible, and this encourages them to become so. Through Circle support, offenders make choices and take actions that build their self-esteem and reintegrate them with their communities.

As those at Roca observed, Circles also empower state, law enforcement, and justice officials to function not only as professionals but also as community members. By speaking from the heart, they become accepted as part of the community and enjoy far greater respect than when they were held apart as experts.

People in the community are empowered by the Circle process as well. In Circles, all of us are invited to take back our collective responsibility and, as a result, to have our perspectives and interests heard. Committed to empowering communities of color in particular, Circle trainer Gwen Chandler-Rhivers reflects on how Circles have impacted her community:

> People of color have always had volunteers come into their community to help them, but people of color have never been volunteers themselves. This Circle work is about empowering people of color, so that they will not only sit at the table but can eat some of what's on it as well. It seems to me that this process works best for those who have been oppressed the most. It gives them an option to make a difference in their communities—a process to begin healing.

Deeply engaged in bringing Circles to African American families and communities, Alice Lynch has observed a similar shift to community empowerment:

> We are so used to others coming into our community under the disguise of trying to take care of us, that when we find a process that will allow us to take care of ourselves, we are suspicious of the process at first. Once we figure it out, though, we become totally committed to the work. In other words, once people are clear that this whole Circle process is about them as individuals and as a community, they totally buy into it. And that's what's happened. We have volunteers who will never miss a

Circle, because they feel the commitment not only to the families but also to the community.

As people use Circles to work through intense emotions, generate mutual support, and develop a sense of community, they feel empowered to face other life challenges with the help of Circles. Carolyn Boyes-Watson describes what happened at Roca when a youth was killed by a car:

> One of the most moving moments for the Roca staff was when young people organized a Circle for themselves in the wake of a tragic death of a young person. Last summer, Desi Kimmon, twelve years old, was killed in a hit-and-run auto accident. People at Roca were devastated, and staff were overwhelmed dealing with the loss. . . . The adult staff simply did not know what to do for the young people at Roca who were already facing so much loss in their lives. Exhausted and emotionally drained themselves, the best the staff hoped for was that not too many young people would show up at Desi's wake. But they did show up—all of them. When it was over, a group of young women, age thirteen, headed over to Roca and demanded a Circle so they could talk about Desi and grieve together.[38]

Angie Rodriguez, the coordinator for Project Victory (an intensive after-school program for youths twelve to fifteen), describes the Circle that followed:

> So then when Desi died, everyone from Project Victory decided to go to room 233 and have a Circle about death and about appreciating people before they die, and how you say, "I love you" to somebody before they die and not

while they are lying in a casket. After the funeral, they came straight to Roca. "Sayra, Angie, we want a Circle, we want to run a Circle. We want to keep a Circle. Give us the candle and a space." Sayra was, like, okay, but you need to have an adult there, so they said, "Angie, can you come?" and I said "Okay, I'll go with you guys." They ran the Circle. They put Desi's picture on the floor, they put all these sacred things. . . . One of the girls put a special thing that was hers because her mother passed away, and they used that as the talking piece. It was really good. And these kids are thirteen . . . running the Circle. They did guidelines on a flip chart with markers, different colors. They burned sage, they took Desi's picture, and put the sage around it, and smudged it. Then they started with an opening and closing. . . . I didn't have to do anything. . . . They just did it.[39]

The Circle process reintroduces participatory democracy

By participating in making decisions that shape the quality of community life, we gain in Circles a concrete experience of democracy—of taking responsibility and having a voice—which goes beyond the more abstract experiences of voting or responding to opinion polls. Circles immerse us in the values and practices of participatory democracy. We experience basic democratic truths; namely, that our views count and that without each of us, some important contribution would be missing. Being radically democratic, Circles offer a way to practice democracy in far fuller measure than we may otherwise have opportunities to do. They give us a chance to flex our participatory muscles and to develop skills essential to a democracy—deep listening; constructive, assertive communication; and collective problem-solving.

Unfortunately, the increasingly nonparticipatory and adversarial nature of society's decision-making processes has caused our participatory skills to atrophy. These trends have gained momentum due to several myths about current civic life—myths that undermine our democratic processes. One is that individuals can't make a difference. Another is that public officials don't need citizen involvement to be effective. Yet another is that the challenges are too complex for laypeople to help with.

Participation in Circles debunks all three myths. Not only can individuals working together in Circles make a difference—that's quickly evident—but also, without community involvement, public decision-making fails to make the difference that's called for. Public officials need community involvement to know both what's going on and what the communities see as viable solutions—solutions that the community wants, believes in, and will work for. As to the issue of complexity, the tragic case of Marcel Jacob indicates that the current system of professionals working separately in their own spheres lacks the capacity to handle complex cases—a capacity that Circles possess through their holistic, systemic approach. One Circle volunteer confronted these myths and saw through them because of her participation in Circles:

> The problems seemed too big. The justice system seemed too big, too difficult to understand. Most of you had college degrees, spoke in a funny language, and seemed too smart for me. I just didn't believe I could get involved or make a difference.
>
> After a few Circles, I began to see things very differently. Each problem, taken one at a time, was something I could handle. And, don't take this personally, but none of you were really, you know, all that smart. In fact, some stuff you did and said were really stupid. You need people like me. People like me could make a difference—as

much of a difference as bringing in more police, more probation people, or even more judges.

As people become involved in securing their community's well-being, it dawns on them that the real force for change lies with them and not with the state. They realize, as this volunteer did, that simply investing more state money and resources won't turn things around. What's needed is for communities to pull together—to build the connections that show them their real power and what they can achieve with it.

Having experienced a true sense of efficacy—of making a difference—within a Circle, most acquire an appetite for more involvement. Community members discover not only how they share some responsibility for what happens, but also that they possess some power to break cycles of hurt. The greater connectedness, understanding, and respect that Circles foster make communities in the long run more able to accept differences and to affirm each person's value within the whole. This ability to hold differences and affirm worth makes our communities safe in ways no control mechanisms can.

Inspired by their experiences in justice Circles, some people are moved to use Circles in other areas of their lives, especially within their own families. One Circle volunteer commented, "I started using Circles in my family after dealing with that case [of domestic violence] in Circle." Right after her initial training in Circles, Gwen Chandler-Rhivers used the process with her family as well:

About four years ago, my daughter's grandmother died. In the car driving to Chicago for the funeral, my daughter angrily started asking me questions about her dad. They had never been in much of a relationship, and it was only because of his mom that they had any ties at all.

So what was going to reinforce that bond between them now? I suggested that she wait until we got to Chicago and ask him herself.

After the funeral, we ended up at my mother's house sitting around the table. I started talking about this useful process that I had learned in Minnesota. It was a way to look at things in a different way—kind of like looking through new eyeglasses. So I took my eyeglasses off and used them to demonstrate how we can look through new eyes. As I talked—there were about ten of us—they looked at me like I just stepped off the moon and told me to take my new process back to Minnesota. They weren't interested.

So I said, "No, listen to me." And I started to talk about how we make assumptions about each other, because we don't take the time to engage in relationships. At that point, my daughter took the eyeglasses away from me and, sort of using them as a microphone, said to her dad, "Why haven't you been involved in my life?" She started asking him all the questions that she had been holding for twenty-seven years.

Dad took the glasses from her and started talking about why he doesn't talk about himself and his feelings. He talked and talked and talked for forty-five minutes. I leaned over to a friend and said, "He's doing it and doesn't even know it."

So he started answering her questions. After seven hours, we were still sitting at the table. He reached into his pocket and pulled out a necklace that he had taken from his mom's body, placed it around her neck, and said, "I want to be your dad—I just don't know how. It's twenty-seven years too late, but I can start today with the help of all the people in this room. I can be the best dad I can, because I do love you."

I leaned over to my friend again and said, "If it can work here, it can work anywhere."

People are also using Circles to deal with different community concerns. For one volunteer, her experience in justice Circles inspired her to get more actively involved in health issues:

> I don't participate in justice Circles, at least not as much anymore. Now I'm into health issues, but I would never be there if I hadn't seen what can be done in Circles when ordinary people like me get involved.

Some organizations now use Circles to encourage participatory decision-making internally. Roca and the Carcross/Tagish First Nation, for example, use Circles for most of their significant internal decisions. In both communities, the commitment to empowering all voices—which using Circles demonstrates—profoundly changed not only the character of the meetings but also the overall institutional culture. One member commented:

> I hated meetings. I would miss as many as I could. I was always anxious to leave. Now I look forward to them, and I'm surprised how quickly the time goes by. Doing it in a Circle gives everyone a chance to have their say. We all learn more, and the stuff that comes out is the stuff that needs to come out to get at the real work we need to do with each other—to work with each other in a good way. The agenda is there, but it isn't the most important thing anymore. What is really important comes out, and it never did before. It stayed in the offices and in whispers. That's what made the meetings dishonest—and difficult. Well, sometimes it's difficult in Circles too, but in a different way. It's a good difficult, because it is honest and safe.

We learn about government and self-government growing up. For many youths, though, democracy isn't what they experience, either at home or at school. Many are not asked to help make the decisions that affect their lives. Decisions and rules are too often handed down to them with the expectation that they simply obey. This top-down approach deprives young people of the experience of democratic participation, i.e., of both the empowerment and the responsibility that go with self-government.

Circles give young people a forum for actually doing democracy. From her extensive experience training young people in Circles, Gwen Chandler-Rhivers observes, "Kids grab onto this process very quickly—much quicker than adults—because their genuine nature wants to help people feel better, and they appreciate both being treated as equals and treating others as equals." Carolyn Boyes-Watson elaborates:

> The experience of being respectfully and fully listened to is one of the most profoundly meaningful elements of the Circle process. In an adult-dominated world, young people are marginalized and voiceless; disadvantaged young people are especially "voiceless" at home, in school, and in the wider community. The Circle process offers [youths] an opportunity for participation as equals that does not exist in any other social context. Participation and empowerment are mutually reinforcing: as the Circle opens a space for democratic participation, young people embrace the Circle process as a healthy and hopeful way to address their own needs and fulfill their own dreams for themselves and their community.[40]

From his work with young people, Vichey Phoung underscores this need:

For kids from the street . . . not too many people stop and ask, "How you doing?" Circles help to do that. . . . For once in their lifetime, they sit in a Circle, and there's a check-in: "How you doing?" . . . "How you feeling?" . . . Young people got so much to say, but they've been neglected for so many years . . . just left out on the street. People don't understand them, parents don't understand them . . . and they're just left out there, and they want to talk to people, and they want to share their stuff, but they don't know how to do it in a good way, and that's what Circles do.[41]

Considering all these gains, the notion of evaluating a Circle based on what happens to an offender misses the point. The success of Circles lies not solely in criminal justice outcomes but in these long-term effects involving personal, community, and cultural change. With time, Circles reduce crime by helping communities heal and grow—by weaving connections that hold people on a good and healing path. Circles are, therefore, as much about community-building as they are about crime. They enable communities to take charge of their fate and make decisions for their own well-being. Circles lay the foundation for creating a sense of community that "does the job," not only in handling crime and preventing it, but also in nurturing all the intangibles that make communities strong and healthy—what we want and hope our communities can be.

Chapter Seven

Tapping Our Powers to Change

What lies behind us and what lies before us are tiny matters compared to what lies within us.

—Ralph Waldo Emerson

When I feel pain, I stop and acknowledge it and celebrate it, because it points in new directions. This has been a painful experience for all of us. I hope that on this road we travel that we take the time to acknowledge the pain of each other and celebrate it, because out of that pain comes opportunities for growth.

—A Circle participant

Healing the legacy of hurt

Hurts happen, so how can we best respond to them? Families and communities can't afford to do nothing—to let offenders, victims, their families, friends, and communities carry around the hurts of crime indefinitely. From both experiencing hurt and observing others struggle with it, we individually and as cultures are learning that holding on to emotional damage isn't healthy. Walls go up, masks go on, misunderstandings escalate, as hearts harden and close. Unhealed wounds fester, causing bad feelings to eat away at people and destroy relationships. Millennia ago, the Gospel of St. Thomas named this danger: "If you fail to bring forth what is within you, what you fail to bring forth will destroy you."

Those we call offenders often prove this point with their lives. Having experienced more pain than they knew how to heal, offenders act out their wounds on others. Unhealed traumas, like unresolved conflicts, endanger the well-being of both individuals and communities. They function like time bombs, ticking and periodically exploding through generations. Does inflicting additional hurt through punishment defuse these bombs or free people from carrying them? When someone is holding more bombs than they know what to do with, will punishment stop them from tossing a few in other people's directions or setting a couple off in their own lives through addictions or other self-destructive behavior?

We all pay the price for letting wounds continue unhealed, since crime changes the character, spirit, and very soul of a community. The families of victims and offenders struggle with an anguish that impedes their capacity to function. Often they do not find the peace that would enable them to move fully beyond the crime. Victims experience a life-shattering pain that can cut to the core of their will to survive. Offenders sooner or later pay a profound price for their crimes as well. Their isolation as well as shame and guilt can drag them down to an alcohol- and drug-addicted life, further dispiriting them and reinforcing their sense of hopelessness.

Beyond these images of face-to-face crime, faceless crimes take their own devastating toll: Enrons and Worldcoms wipe out life savings and pensions; accumulating levels of toxins in our environment and bodies bring dangerous consequences that we cannot fully know; and collusion between government and business steals from the public good, diminishing our freedom. St. Thomas was right: either we face what is unhealed within us and within our systems, or what is within us will destroy us.

"Bringing forth what is within us"

If keeping wounds hidden and unhealed brings pain upon pain, then the cure is to bring forth what's inside. Circles provide a safe and uncontaminated space where this can happen—where inner wounds can be opened and cleaned, so they can begin to heal. The Gospel of St. Thomas suggests precisely this remedy: "If you bring forth what is within you, what you bring forth will save you."

To air what lies within, Circles engage both the outward and the inward dimensions of who we are. Outwardly, Circles bring us together as equals—fellow human beings whose only common bond at first may be that of having lived through the same experience of crime but from opposite perspectives. Circles build on the truth of our relatedness. No one exists in isolation—a fact that violence and crime painfully underscore.

Pain tells us that our relatedness needs tending. Something isn't working in how we're connecting, whether as individuals, families, communities, or a society, and we need to look deeper than the surface of breakdown to see what's wrong. Rather than lessening our connectedness by sending people off to prison and letting the state make the hard moral decisions that crime raises, communities can use crime to strengthen bonds. They can bring people together to work things out in a good way.

In this endeavor, Circles do what courts can't. Courts focus on the facts and circumstances of a case—the outer side. Yet these outer facts can't be changed: what's done is done. What makes the greatest difference in healing and transformation is a shift in our inner experience. Circles intentionally create spaces where such shifts can happen. We listen to each other deeply and from our hearts, which inspires mutual respect and understanding. Profound listening also inspires deeper levels of emotional processing. We experience compassion for ourselves and empathy for others, which moves us to right wrongs insofar as we're able. By drawing on the inward, Circles give us space to move, shift, change, adjust, adapt, and through it all, to grow. Together, we gradually birth a wider sense of our lives and communities.

In other words, by shifting the focus to what's inside, Circles

generate a faith in our human potentials to heal and be transformed. We each have capacities for good yet to be tapped. Pain
can be a doorway to tapping them by making us look inside,
where our greatest powers reside. Circles create a space where we
can both share our pain and experience ourselves and each other
as more, and accessing this "more" can have a profoundly healing,
transforming effect.

Just as pain came from our relatedness, so healing and transformation come from experiencing our relatedness in new ways.
Healing and transformation seem to be processes that are hard for
us to do alone. To experience ourselves as fully alive again—to feel
our hearts open enough to start breathing through pain—we need
help. We're more able to "bring forth what is within us" safely—to
express what we're feeling, even if it's raw and wrenching emotions—when we do this together. Supported by the Circle space,
we learn how to share hurts openly, without an intention to hurt
back. We let others see inside, and in so doing, we see inside ourselves. Circles hold the inner lives of all participants equally in a
good way—respectfully, compassionately—and this way of being
held enables us to access inner capacities we didn't know we had.

Creating alternative public spaces

If our potentials remain unseen and untapped, it's because we're
not often "held" in such a fashion. The spaces we inhabit in the
dominant culture—schools, workplaces, professions, the justice
system, and sometimes even marriages, families, and religions—
too frequently hold us in judgments and punishments, not in
respect and compassion. Since childhood, we have lived under
a judge-and-punish model, which is as much a philosophy as
a practice. The framework is culture-wide, and the message it
sends isn't about honoring intrinsic worth but about wielding
external control through negative labeling or threats of rejec-

tion. We're told that if we fall short in any way, we'll no longer be considered worthy.

Held in this threatening framework, we construct defenses that hide our inner being. Afraid of being judged or punished, we don't access our full powers to act from our most open or generous selves. We don't behave this way as our first choice; we do it because of how our systems work and because of how we feel when we're in them. Retreating into shells is how we've learned to survive.

Circles send a completely different message. Through the Circle space, we begin to experience how we can be with each other differently, without the fears and defenses that the judge-and-punish framework instills in us. We learn that we can bring our best energies to each other, instead of our most anguished, conflicted, or sharp edged. Experiencing a Circle way of being together, especially around hurts and conflicts, we gain hope that our relationships can thrive. Instead of fearing conflict, we begin to trust that we can work things out in healing and mutually supportive ways.

Not that Circles can work in all cases. As we said in the beginning, they're not a panacea. Some people may be so wounded that they can't access their better selves, even in Circles. Circles can't undo in a few gatherings what severely unhealthy relationships, families, and societies have done to people for decades or generations. But they can offer an alternative way of being together, and for many, experiencing this alternative opens possibilities and plants hope.

A closing reflection

All of us carry wounds within us. They're part of our humanity. In ordinary life, we walk around wanting to touch one another, and yet we feel as if our arms are strapped to our sides. Our experiences, especially our painful ones, restrict our ability to reach out to each other in the ways our hearts long to do.

Sometimes in a Circle, though, the crisis of crime or serious conflict tears loose these restrictions, and we're able to reach for one another, perhaps tentatively, awkwardly, stiffly at first, but nonetheless authentically. Circles provide the space in which we reveal ourselves, uncover our core humanity, and allow others to feel, know, and touch us. We can't walk through the sacred space of Circles and emerge as we were. We're deepened, and from those depths, we find the power to create our worlds anew—together.

> As the story unfolds,
> The labels fall away.
> Tears blend.
> The "other" becomes one of us.
> We cannot hold the other separate, for
> We are inextricably intertwined in a combined story.

Notes

1. William Isaacs, *Dialogue and the Art of Thinking Together: A Pioneering Approach to Communicating in Business and in Life* (New York: Doubleday Currency, 1999), xvi.

2. Caroline A. Westerhoff, "Conflict: The Birthing of the New," in *Conflict Management in Congregations,* ed. David B. Lott (Bethesda: The Alban Institute, 2001), 54–61. The article was originally published in *Action Information* 12, no. 3 (May/June 1986): 1–5.

3. For accounts of Priscilla's story, see: *AMICUS Outreach,* Winter 2001, 3. Also: Rubén Rosario, "Abused Teenager Becomes 'Million-Dollar Kid,'" *Saint Paul Pioneer Press,* 21 and 22 April 2002.

4. Dr. Carolyn Boyes-Watson, *Holding the Space: The Journey of Circles at Roca* (unpublished report, The Center for Restorative Justice at Suffolk University, Boston, Massachusetts, October 2002), hereafter referred to as the Roca Report, 4–5.

5. Roca Report, 37.

6. Ibid., 40.

7. Ibid., 14–15.

8. Judie Bopp, Michael Bopp, Lee Brown, and Phil Lane Jr., *The Sacred Tree: Reflections on Native American Spirituality,* 3d ed. (Twin Lakes, Wis.: Lotus Light Publications, 1989), 80.

9. Kathy Burns, "System of Justice," *Mille Lacs County Times* (Milaca, Minnesota) 25 June 1998, pp. 3, 8.

10. Roca Report, 26.

11. G. Cormick, N. Dale, P. Emonds, G. Sigurdson, and B. Stuart, *Building Consensus for a Sustainable Future* (Ottawa: National Round Table, 1996). This work discusses how some of these principles apply to conflicts centered around the economy and the environment.

12. Roca Report, 31.

13. Ibid.

14. Ibid., 33.

15. Ibid.

16. His Holiness the Dalai Lama, *Ethics for the New Millennium* (New York: Riverhead Books, Penguin Putnam, 1999), 22.

17. Ibid., 23.

18. Bopp, Bopp, Brown, and Lane, *The Sacred Tree,* 32.

19. Ibid., 33, 35.

20. Roca Report, 8.

21. Margaret J. Wheatley, "Good Listening," *IONS Noetic Sciences Review: Exploring the Frontiers of Consciousness,* no. 60 (June–August 2002): 14–16. Adapted from Margaret J. Wheatley, *Turning to One Another: Simple Conversations to Restore Hope to the Future* (Los Angeles: Berrett-Koehler Publishers, 2002).

22. Roca Report, 14.

23. Ibid., 15.

24. Ibid., 10–11.

25. Ibid., 41.

26. Ibid., 40.

27. Ibid., 38, 36.

28. Ibid., 36.

29. Ibid.

30. *See:* Roca Report, 37.

31. *See:* Alfie Kohn, *Punished by Rewards: The Trouble with Gold Stars, Incentive Plans, A's, Praise, and Other Bribes* (Boston and New York: Houghton Mifflin Company, 1993).

32. Rubén Rosario, "Abused Teenager Becomes 'Million-Dollar Kid.'"

33. Roca Report, 7.

34. Ibid., 26, 27.

35. Ibid., 25.

36. Peter Senge, *The Fifth Discipline: The Art and Practice of the Learning Organization* (New York: Doubleday Currency, 1990), 6, 7.

37. Quoted in David La Chapelle, "Trusting the Web of Life," *IONS: Noetic Sciences Review: Exploring the Frontiers of Consciousness,* June–August 2001, Number 56, 17.

38. Roca Report, 20.

39. Ibid., 20–21.

40. Ibid., 12.

41. Ibid, 13.

Acknowledgments

WE THANK THE STAFF OF LIVING JUSTICE PRESS for helping us with the very difficult challenge of translating our experiences into this publication. Denise Breton shook this work loose from our timorous hands. Her tireless editing and her commitment to finding a way to move this from our "to do" pile into the hands of people seeking to know more about peacemaking Circles inspired and helped us finish what seemed never to have a finishing point.

We express our deep gratitude to the First Nation Elders, community members, justice professionals, and so many others who have been pioneers, teachers, and guides on this journey. We are also deeply indebted to the courageous Circle participants who have proved the power of opening our hearts to each other, even when it seems impossible to do.

We each feel deep gratitude to so many for the insights and stories that fill this book and for helping us on our personal journeys in the practice of Circles. The nature of our work has brought countless people into our lives, and each person has contributed to our development. As a result, we want to acknowledge that our long journeys have been filled with many guides who have shared their wisdom, love, and passion with us. They have also offered support and forgiveness when we failed to understand. We have needed all of our guides and all of their gifts.

To honor where we are today, we have named only those who helped us start the journey of using peacemaking Circles to deal with crime. But in thanking those who launched us on this path, we also remember with abiding affection those who continue to sustain us on our journeys—and there are so many. The adaptation of Circles to dealing with crime that we have presented in this book first grew from Barry's work with multiparty conflict resolution and later from his work as a judge. Consequently, those named from the early years came from his experiences:

In the 1970s, several Papua New Guineans revealed for me the power inherent in traditional community-based methods of resolving differences. Later, Northern First Nation communities in Canada continued these revelations. People in all these places launched me on my journey.

In Papua New Guinea, Mek Taylor, Moi Avei, Rabbi Namaliu, Bernard Naracobi, Nahou Rooney, and Rose Kekado challenged my thinking about conflict.

In Yukon communities, many helped me to begin the work of using Circles to deal with crime: in Carcross, Ilene Walley, Dora Wedge, Johnny Johns, Pete Sidney, Harold Gatensby, Colleen James, and Annie Auston; in Haines Junction, James Allen, Barb and Chuck Hume, Joan Graham, and Kathy and Sheila Kushniruk; in Burwash Landing, Joe Johnston, Robin Bradasch, Grace Chambers, Louise Bouvier, and Shawn Allen; in Kwanlin Dun, Rose Wilson, Rose Rowlands, Jessie Scarf, John Edzerza, Yvonne Smarch, Sofie Smarch, Edwin Scurvey, and Leonard Gordon; and in Carmacks, Elizabeth Anderson, Velma Albert, Joseph O'Brien, and Roddy Blackjack. Each in their own ways, these people were there at the beginning.

Ingeborg and Hans Mohr and the Howe Island family in Ontario have been there for me in so many ways from even before the beginning. They made it necessary for me to ask essential questions and to pursue the possible changes that these essential questions demand.

Beginning in the late 1990s, Nares Mountain Wilderness Camp in Yukon introduced peacemaking Circles to people from all over the world. I still carry the initial spirit and experiences of this place and the people who came as a constant reminder of the potential of Circles. Its founding pioneers—Harold Gatensby, Colleen James, Phil Gatensby, and Stuart Breithaupt—had a vision that persists. This vision permeates most of the work with Circles in the justice system.

Supporting Community Initiatives— Barry's Thoughts on Funding

The need for community-led justice initiatives

When, as a judge, I first began asking communities to become involved in sharing responsibility for crime, I made, among others, two very significant mistakes. First, I tried to discover ways to bring the community into the justice system. To a limited extent this is a progressive step. However, the more important step is to bring the justice system into the community—that is, to engage the justice system in responding to the needs of the community rather than to ask the community to respond to the needs of the justice system. The justice system should do what communities cannot or do not want to do, rather than merely enlisting the communities to do what the justice system does not want to do.

Many community justice initiatives are not community based or led. They're based within the justice system and led by the justice system. Accordingly, they bring the community into the justice system. In these initiatives, the values and objectives of the justice agencies prevail. Though this is not necessarily a bad thing, it's simply not enough—not enough to profoundly change how we address crime. If community justice initiatives are based on justice system values and led by justice professionals, the community provides an alternative method for pursuing justice system objectives. The arrangement doesn't provide an alternative way for either to realize a different set of objectives—community objectives. If these initiatives are led by justice professionals, invaluable contributions that communities can make are often neither fully sought nor respected.

Circles, to be fully effective, need to be based in and led by the community. Circles offer the basis for forming a genuine partnership among all state agencies and the community, but it's a partnership that operates on community values and objectives. Many of my early initiatives were led by the court and based on our systems' values. This was my first mistake.

The need for adequate funding

This first mistake set up my second. When I shifted to supporting community-led processes, I expected these processes to be carried fully on the backs of volunteers. Mistake. Community processes need funding, training, and staff to be effective. While volunteers must lead the process, they cannot take on all the responsibilities that come with the work of Circles. If volunteers are to step up and assume significant responsibility, they need staff, resources, and training. Without this support, they're reduced to glorified gofers for justice professionals. Moreover, the support must be significant; otherwise Circles and other similar community initiatives are set up to fail.

That successful community justice initiatives are forced to close their doors or reduce their work because of a lack of support, while many mainstream justice programs—clearly documented as failures—continue to be funded makes no sense. In the justice system, though, success isn't the basis of securing funding. Mainstream practices prevail over new, successful community initiatives, because there is no voice for the community in the budgetary process and because historical funding patterns are controlled by many vested interests that cling to established practices, even when such practices are long-proven failures.

We don't need to spend more public funds on criminal justice. We need to invest these funds for the first time according to some criteria other than past practices. We need to invest wisely in work that actually makes a difference. This means cutting back significantly in what formal justice agencies do alone and instead investing much more both in what justice agencies do with communities and in what communities do alone.

Experience worldwide attests to the wisdom of this shift. The less a community is involved, the more we depend on professional responses to crime—responses that are expensive and questionably effective. Informal community controls, by contrast, are consistently less expensive and far more effective. As communities discover their power and start organizing, we have the opportunity to support these growing community-based efforts. To do this, though, we must change the flow of public investment, and that won't be easy.

Ideas for generating funding

The Circle processes described in this book have been carried out in many places with little or no funding. Despite their successes on many fronts, some of these initiatives have been forced to reduce their workloads or close their doors due to lack of funding. Now many of these communities are beginning to craft creative ways to change funding patterns. Here are a few that I have seen work and that you may want to consider for your community.

Swap community time for jail time: not doing time but doing good. In Bend, Oregon, for example, when community programs reduce the number of juveniles being sent to jail, these local justice programs receive the funds that otherwise would have been spent to incarcerate the juveniles. The young people are not "doing time" but "doing good." That is, rather than spend time in jail, they're actively involved in important, constructive community projects, which gives them a chance to pay back the community, regain their self-esteem, work with potential employers, and gain marketable skills. Dennis Maloney, who helped initiate this program, reports that it has resulted in a 72 percent drop in the number of juveniles incarcerated from the county.

Earning their way. When community justice initiatives reduce crime and related social costs, they're seldom given credit for doing so, and the savings are silently sucked back into government coffers. To measure the savings, a community could use the year before a community justice initiative begins as the benchmark to calculate the per capita costs of delivering justice system services, related services, and other social costs stemming directly or indirectly from crime. Then, if after two years the costs are less, all or at least half of the savings to government could be given to the community justice initiative whose work has generated the savings. In doing so, the community justice committee earns its keep, gains a clear measure of the impact of its work, and possesses the funds to make further initiatives to advance community objectives.

Tax incentives. When citizens donate money to a charity, they're given tax reductions. Why not allow tax reductions for the time citizens donate to community justice initiatives?

Corporate job incentives. As part of their charitable and community outreach programs, corporations could grant employees paid time for them to donate to community justice initiatives.

State agency recognition. Hiring preferences, merit increases, and promotions within justice agencies should substantially recognize the time public servants spend working on community justice initiatives. Why not give community justice committees input on public servant performance assessments? Why not lend paid public servants to community justice initiatives, so that the government provides some staff support?

There are many more outside-the-box ideas for supporting community justice initiatives, but, in my view, they should include direct and significant government funding. Much of this funding can come from reducing our excessive reliance on state agencies. If we want community involvement, we need to invest public funds in it. The returns are invaluable on many levels.

Asserting our citizens' right of choice over how we resolve conflicts and crime

A fundamental democratic right lies at the core of these issues: our right to choose how we respond to conflicts and crime. Each citizen should be able to choose between state services and community-based services. If a community respects constitutional protections and offers a safe place to address crime in ways that incorporate larger public objectives, a community justice initiative should operate as a matter of right to provide services to any citizen who chooses the community process.

Currently, citizens don't get to decide how a crime is dealt with. If it's the pleasure of police, probation officers, or judges to send cases to the community, then the community justice committees receive cases to work on. Further, if it's within the pleasure of local justice agencies to fund community justice initiatives, then the community justice committees have resources to do the work that the state allows. Yet why should community justice initiatives exist at the pleasure of the state? We need to provide communities with both the resources and the authority to resolve crime by working in partnership with the justice system.

It's contrary to democracy for the state to hold a monopoly over how we resolve conflicts and crime, yet our entrenched spending patterns establish precisely that. State justice agencies and courts receive guaranteed public support of immense sums, while community justice initiatives struggle year to year to garner a relative pittance. The disparity secures the formal system's virtual monopoly over how we respond to crime.

Circles provide an essential and direct means for citizens to challenge this monopoly by expanding our options. Through Circles, we take on the responsibilities of democratic citizenship. The well-being not only of our democracy but also of our communities depend on our involvement. That being so, we must find the means to fund community justice work, so that the alternatives we create can endure and grow.

Books That Have Lit Our Paths

Arrien, Angeles. *The Four-Fold Way: Walking the Paths of the Warrior, Teacher, Healer, and Visionary.* New York: Harper Collins, 1993.

Baldwin, Christina. *Calling The Circle: The First and Future Culture.* Newberg, Or.: Swan-Raven Company, 1994; reprint New York: Bantam Doubleday Dell, 1998.

Bolen, Jean Shinoda. *The Millionth Circle—How to Change Ourselves and the World: The Essential Guide to Women's Circles.* Berkeley, Calif.: Conari Press, 1999.

Bopp, Judie, Michael Bopp, Lee Brown, and Phil Lane Jr. *The Sacred Tree: Reflections on Native American Spirituality.* Lethbridge, Alberta, Canada: Four Worlds International Institute, 1984.

Boyes-Watson, Carolyn. *Holding the Space: The Journey of Circles at Roca.* Boston, Mass.: The Center for Restorative Justice at Suffolk University, 2002.

Breton, Denise, and Stephen Lehman. *The Mystic Heart of Justice: Restoring Wholeness in a Broken World.* West Chester, Pa.: Chrysalis Books, Swedenborg Foundation, 2001.

Casarjian, Robin. *Houses of Healing: A Prisoner's Guide to Inner Power and Freedom.* Boston: The Lionheart Foundation, 1995.

The Dalai Lama. *Ethics for the New Millennium.* New York: Riverhead Books, Penguin Putnam, 1999.

Engel, Beverly. *Women Circling the Earth: A Guide to Fostering Community, Healing, and Empowerment.* Deerfield Beach, Fla.: Health Communications, 2000.

Garfield, Charles, Cindy Spring, and Sedonia Cahill. *Wisdom Circles: A Guide to Self-Discovery and Community Building in Small Groups.* New York: Hyperion, 1998.

Herman, Judith. *Trauma and Recovery: The Aftermath of Violence—From Domestic Abuse to Political Terror.* New York: Basic Books, 1992.

hooks, bell. *All About Love: New Visions.* New York: William Morrow and Company, 2000.

Isaacs, William. *Dialogue and the Art of Thinking Together: A Pioneering Approach to Communicating in Business and in Life.* New York: Doubleday Currency, 1999.

Kohn, Alfie. *Punished by Rewards: The Trouble with Gold Stars, Incentive Plans, A's, Praise, and Other Bribes.* Boston and New York: Houghton Mifflin Company, 1993.

_____. *No Contest: The Case Against Competition.* Boston: Houghton Mifflin Company, 1987.

Lucado, Max. *You Are Special.* Illustrations by Sergio Martinez. Wheaton, Ill.: Crossway Books, a Division of Good News Publishers, 1997.

McKnight, John. *The Careless Society: Community and Its Counterfeits.* New York: Basic Books, 1996.

Miller, Rhea Y. *Cloudhand Clenched Fist: Chaos, Crisis, and the Emergence of Community.* San Diego, Calif.: LuraMedia, 1996.

Mohr, Hans. *Atonement: At-one-ment.* Howe Island, Ontario, Canada: Howe Island Writings, unpublished, completed 1996, revised 2002.

Mountain Dreamer, Oriah. *The Invitation.* New York: Harper Collins, 1999.

Nhat Hanh, Thich. *Peace Is Every Step: The Path of Mindfulness in Everyday Life.* New York: Bantam Books, 1991.

_____. *Anger: Wisdom for Cooling the Flames.* New York: Riverhead Books, Penguin Putnam, 2001.

Putnam, Robert D. *Bowling Alone: The Collapse and Revival of American Community.* Carmichael, Calif.: Touchstone Books, 2001.

Ross, Rupert. *Returning to the Teachings: Exploring Aboriginal Justice.* Toronto, Ontario, Canada: Penguin Books Canada, 1996.

Senge, Peter. *The Fifth Discipline: The Art and Practice of the Learning Organization*. New York: Doubleday Currency, 1990.

Stone, Douglas, Bruce Patton, and Sheila Heen. *Difficult Conversations: How to Discuss What Matters Most*. New York: Viking Penguin, 1999.

Sullivan, Dennis, and Larry Tifft. *Restorative Justice: Healing the Foundations of Our Everyday Lives*. Monsey, N.Y.: Willow Tree Press, 2001.

Van Ness, Daniel, and Karen Heetderks Strong. *Restoring Justice*. Cincinnati, Ohio: Anderson Publishing Company, 1997.

Weeks, Dudley. *The Eight Essential Steps of Conflict Resolution: Preserving Relationships at Work, at Home, and in the Community*. New York: Tarcher/Putnam, 1992.

Wheatley, Margaret J. *Turning to One Another: Simple Conversations to Restore Hope to the Future*. San Francisco, Calif.: Berrett-Koehler, 2002.

White Deer of Autumn. *Ceremony: In the Circle of Life*. Illustrations by Daniel San Souci. Hillsboro, Oreg.: Beyond Words Publishing, 1983.

Zehr, Howard. *Changing Lenses: A New Focus for Crime and Justice*. Scottdale, Pa.: Herald Press, 1990.

_____. *The Little Book of Restorative Justice*. Intercourse, Pa.: Good Books, 2002.

Zimmerman, Jack, in collaboration with Virginia Coyle. *The Way of Council*. Las Vegas, Nev.: Bramble Books, 1996.

Index

A

aboriginal societies, xi–xiii, 68–70, 76. *See also* ancient wisdom, First Nations, indigenous

accountability, 10, 12–13, 67, 153; and follow-up, 128, 153, 199; and implementing Circle consensus, 199–208; and offenders, 12, 21, 35, 40, 59, 177, 207, 228; Circles foster, 67, 113–14; individual and collective, 12–13; shared, 203, 211; to the Circle, 200, 220

addiction, 122, 166, 170, 171, 187–88, 190, 194, 240

adjournment, advantages of: for a break, 178, 189; for clarifying the consensus, 189–92; for forming a consensus, 188–89; for gathering information, 160

African Americans, 117, 149, 150, 161, 187, 229

AMICUS, 22

ancient wisdom, xi–xiii, 33, 49, 68–70

Angelo, Dr. Thomas, 183

applicant, xiii, 171, 177, 179, 184–85, 198, 206; suitability for the Circle process, 158–67

B

balance, 68–69, 70, 72–73, 75. *See also* Medicine Wheel

Baldwin, Molly, 52

Barlow, Ellen, 150

Baylor, Byrd, 65

BIHA, 117

Bolen, Jean Shinoda, 56

Bopp, Judie, 76

Bopp, Michael, 76

Boyes-Watson, Dr. Carolyn, 84, 114, 211, 220, 230–31

breaks, 109–110, 112–13, 145, 186; and consensus, 188–89; and keepers, 88–90. *See also* time

Brown, Lee, 76

B.V.M. Restorative Justice Ministry, 24

C

Carcross/Tagish First Nation, xv, 34, 69, 235

case examples, 3–6, 15–16, 43, 44–45, 59–60, 75, 77–78, 78–79, 91–92, 154–55, 187–88, 191, 201–202, 218–19, 230–31, 233–35

cases: how to get, 151–52

ceremonies: closing, 118–19, 146, 196; of Circles, 28, 82, 115–20; of courts, 119–20; of reintegration, 25–28; opening, 116–18, 133, 135–36, 181

Chandler-Rhivers, Gwen, 138, 187–88, 229, 233–35, 236

as sacred spaces, 32, 49, 65–67, 98, 112, 136, 137, 207, 244; as safe spaces, 17, 31–33, 84, 221, 240–41; as strengthening communities, 13–14, 20, 209; core values of, 33–47; direct participation in, 58–60; elements of, 7–8, 31, 125; for sentencing, *see* sentencing Circles; guidelines for, *see* guidelines; healing power of, 6–7; history of, xi–xii; holistic character of, 39, 62–64, 72, 76, 91, 191, 221, 227–28, 232; keepers of, *see* keepers; phases of, 130–47; physical dimensions of, 131–32; premises of, 9–10; principles of, *see* Circle principles; types of, 50, 128–29, 130, 143, 144, 233, 235; voluntary nature of, 57–58, 115, 164. *See also* Circle process, peacemaking Circles, sentencing Circles

closing phase, 145–46, 195–96; and closing ceremonies, 118–19

Cohen, Judge Larry, 150

committees: Circle organizing committee, 39–40, 50, 54–55, 62, 68, 150; community Circle/justice committee, 55, 61, 132, 149–52, 158–67, 185, 254–55

community: and accountability, 12–13, 220; and broad-based participation and support, 63, 150–52, 175, 203, 226; and benefits to from Circles, 209–215, 220–21, 224–25, 228–29, 233; and ceremonies, 82, 116–17, 136; and Circles as producing

lasting changes in, 13, 209–214, 237; and consensus, 123; and dealing with addiction, 166, 187–88, 190, 194, 206; and designing Circle process, 149–67; and guidelines, 112; and handling logistics, 131; and healing of, 224; and increasing self-reliance of, 13–14, 199, 208; and measuring success and failure, 205–208; and safety, 11; and sentencing, 187–88; and starting a Circle initiative, 149–51; and unresolved crimes in, 111; and voice as "third party," 145; as basis for getting cases, 152; as guided by shared vision, 60; capacity, 157–58; defined, xiv–xv; empowering, 88, 228–31, 233, 235, 237; reintegration, 25–28; relations with justice professionals, 27, 37, 150–51, 165, 232, 255; relations with offenders, 25–26, 40, 41–42, 44–45, 57–58, 59, 162–63, 187–88, 200–201, 202, 206; relations with victims, 163–64, 170, *see also* victims; volunteers, *see* volunteers

community-building, 67–68, 140–41, 209–14, 237; and Circle sentencing, 176–77, 183–84, 204; and Circle training as means for, 23, 57, 266; and empowerment, 233; and inclusivity, 39; and keepers' role, 84, 93; and purpose of Circles, 130, 133–34; and relationships, 140–41, 209–15; as aim of Circles,

About the Authors

Kay Pranis is a national leader in restorative justice, specializing in peacemaking Circles. She served as the Restorative Justice Planner for the Minnesota Department of Corrections from 1994 to 2003. She has also written and presented papers on peacemaking Circles in the United States, Canada, Australia, and Japan. Since 1998, Kay has conducted Circle trainings in a diverse range of communities—from schools to prisons to workplaces to churches, from rural farm towns in Minnesota to Chicago's South Side.

Barry Stuart, a judge of the Territorial Court of the Yukon (now retired), a faculty member of numerous Canadian law schools, and an internationally respected leader in multiparty conflict resolution, has pioneered the use of peacemaking Circles for public processes in Canada and North America over the last twenty years.

Mark Wedge brings a lifelong knowledge of aboriginal culture and broad experience in both using and training others in using peacemaking Circles for complex issues. He carries the Circle process to workplace and public forums, including the outstanding issues in Canada between victims of Mission School abuse and the Anglican Church.

Contact Us

Kay, Barry, and Mark would like to hear from you about your experiences with Circles. They also invite feedback about the book. Please contact them at the following addresses:

Kay Pranis
249 Hamline Avenue South, St. Paul, MN 55105
United States;
e-mail: KayPranis@msn.com; tel. (651) 698-9181

Barry Stuart
e-mail: BDStuart@telus.net; tel. (604) 733-5790

Mark Wedge
Box 12, Tagish, Yukon Y0B 1T0 Canada;
e-mail: MWWedge@yahoo.ca; tel. (867) 399-3507

If this information is out of date, please contact Living Justice Press for current author information.

Kay, Barry, and Mark have been involved in a wide variety of trainings themselves and can also provide information about other training opportunities. They conduct Circle trainings for schools, workplaces, and churches as well as provide coaching and technical assistance in the use of Circles. These trainings have been effective in supporting community building, organizational development, tribal governance, as well as criminal justice uses.

Kay, Barry, and Mark have requested that their royalties from this book go to charitable causes; they have received no money for this publication.

About Living Justice Press

A nonprofit publisher serving the restorative justice movement

Living Justice Press (LJP) seeks to increase public awareness of the principles and practice of restorative justice through book publishing and related media channels, thereby fostering a larger rethinking of what justice means in every aspect of our lives—from home to school to work to courts of law. We strive to create books that are accessible and useful to individuals, families, and community groups as well as to professionals in the field. To this end, LJP is committed to publishing books that are clearly written, attractively produced, affordably priced, and responsive to the information needs of all those interested in the restorative justice movement.

To achieve these goals, however, we need your help:

- Do you have restorative justice stories and experiences that may help and inspire others?
- Do you know people who may want to learn more about restorative justice?
- What critical areas of restorative justice should future LJP publications address?

Thank you for the time and thought you have given to this book. We'd love to hear your ideas about it and other restorative justice matters, and we invite you to join the Living Justice Press community by adding your name to our mailing list. We also hope you'll tell your friends and colleagues about us.

We look forward to hearing from you.

2093 Juliet Avenue, St. Paul, MN 55105
Tel. (651) 695-1008 • Fax. (651) 695-8564
E-mail: info@livingjusticepress.org
Website: www.livingjusticepress.org